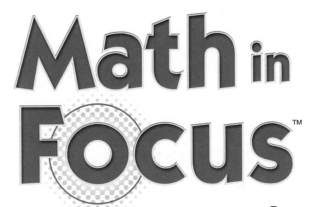

Math in Focus™

Singapore Math
by Marshall Cavendish

Student Book

4B

Consultant and Author
Dr. Fong Ho Kheong

Authors
Chelvi Ramakrishnan and Gan Kee Soon

U.S. Consultants
Dr. Richard Bisk, Andy Clark,
and Patsy F. Kanter

Marshall Cavendish
Education

GREAT★
SOURCE®
HOUGHTON MIFFLIN HARCOURT
Supplemental Publishers

© 2009 Marshall Cavendish International (Singapore) Private Limited

Published by Marshall Cavendish Education
An imprint of Marshall Cavendish International (Singapore) Private Limited
Times Centre, 1 New Industrial Road, Singapore 536196
Customer Service Hotline: (65) 6411 0820
E-mail: tmesales@sg.marshallcavendish.com
Website: www.marshallcavendish.com/education

Distributed by
Great Source
A division of Houghton Mifflin Harcourt Publishing Company
181 Ballardvale Street
P.O. Box 7050
Wilmington, MA 01887-7050
Tel: 1-800-289-4490
Website: www.greatsource.com

First published 2009
Reprinted 2010, 2011

Marshall Cavendish and *Math in Focus™* are trademarks of Times Publishing Limited.

Great Source ® is a registered trademark of Houghton Mifflin Harcourt Publishing Company.

Math in Focus Grade 4 Student Book B
ISBN 978-0-669-01083-1

Printed in United States of America

3 4 5 6 7 8   1897   16 15 14 13 12 11
4500284131   B C D E

Contents

7 Decimals

Look for **Practice and Problem Solving**

Student Book A and Student Book B	Workbook A and Workbook B
• **Let's Practice** in every lesson	• **Independent Practice** for every lesson
• **Put on Your Thinking Cap!** in every chapter	• **Put on Your Thinking Cap!** in every chapter

Look for **Assessment Opportunities**

Student Book A and Student Book B	Workbook A and Workbook B
• **Quick Check** at the beginning of every chapter to assess chapter readiness	• **Cumulative Reviews** six times during the year
• **Guided Practice** after every example or two to assess readiness to continue lesson	• **Mid-Year and End-of-Year Reviews** to assess test readiness
• **Chapter Review/Test** in every chapter to review or test chapter material	

8 Adding and Subtracting Decimals

9 Angles

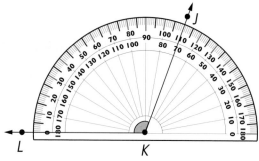

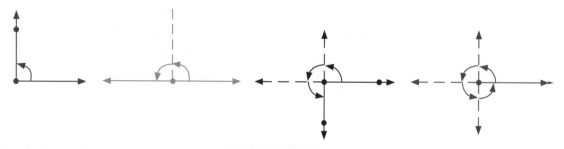

10 Perpendicular and Parallel Line Segments

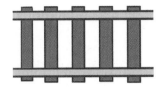

Squares and Rectangles

 **Area and Perimeter**

 **Symmetry**

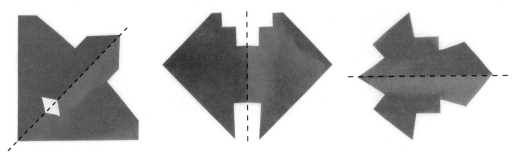

Tessellations

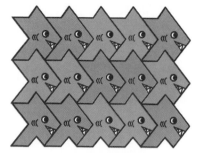

Welcome to

Math in Focus™

This exciting math program comes to you all the way from the country of Singapore. We are sure you will enjoy learning math with the interesting lessons you'll find in these books.

What makes *Math in Focus*™ different?

▶ **Two books** You don't write in the ▭ in this textbook. This book has a matching **Workbook**. When you see the pencil icon 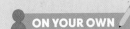, you will write in the **Workbook**.

▶ **Longer lessons** Some lessons may last more than a day, so you can really understand the math.

▶ **Math will make sense** Learn to use bar models to solve word problems with ease.

In this book, look for

Learn	Guided Practice	Let's Practice	ON YOUR OWN
This means you will learn something new.	Your teacher will help you try some sample problems.	You practice what you've learned to solve more problems. You can make sure you really understand.	Now you get to practice with lots of different problems in your own **Workbook**.

Also look forward to *Games, Hands-On Activities, Math Journals, Let's Explore,* and *Put on Your Thinking Cap!*
You will combine logical thinking with math skills and concepts to meet new problem-solving challenges. You will be talking math, thinking math, doing math, and even writing about doing math.

What's in the Workbook?

Math in Focus ™ will give you time to learn important new concepts and skills and check your understanding. Then you will use the practice pages in the **Workbook** to try:

► Solving different problems to practice the new math concept you are learning. In the textbook, keep an eye open for this symbol **ON YOUR OWN**. That will tell you which pages to use for practice.

► *Put on Your Thinking Cap!*

   Challenging Practice problems invite you to think in new ways to solve harder problems.

   Problem Solving challenges you to use different strategies to solve problems.

► Math Journal activities ask you to think about thinking, and then write about that!

Students in Singapore have been using this kind of math program for many years.
Now you can too — are you ready?

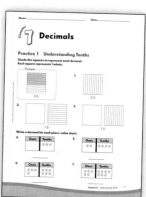

Decimals

BIG IDEAS

▶ Decimals are another way to show amounts that are parts of a whole.

▶ A decimal has a decimal point to the right of the ones place and digits to the right of the decimal point.

1

Knowing fractions with a denominator of 10

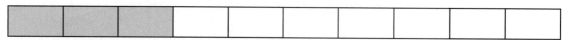

The shaded parts show $\frac{3}{10}$. Read $\frac{3}{10}$ as three tenths.

Knowing mixed numbers with a denominator of 10

The shaded parts show $\frac{23}{10}$ or $2\frac{3}{10}$. Read $2\frac{3}{10}$ as two and three tenths.

Expressing fractions as equivalent fractions with a denominator of 10, and simplifying fractions with a denominator of 10

$$\frac{3}{5} \overset{\times 2}{\underset{\times 2}{=}} \frac{6}{10}$$

$$\frac{8}{10} \overset{\div 2}{\underset{\div 2}{=}} \frac{4}{5}$$

Multiply the numerator and denominator by the same number.

Divide the numerator and denominator by the same number.

Rounding numbers to the nearest ten

When the ones digit is 0, 1, 2, 3, or 4, round the number to the lesser ten.

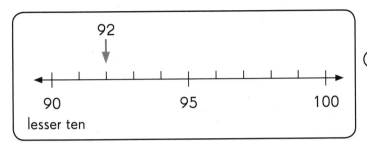

92 is nearer to 90 than to 100.

92 is about 90.

When the ones digit is 5, 6, 7, 8, or 9, round the number to the greater ten.

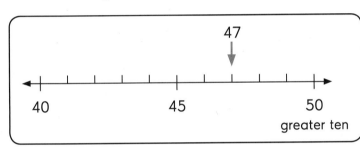

47 is nearer to 50 than to 40.

47 is about 50.

✔ Quick Check

Find the fraction or mixed number shown by the shaded parts.

1 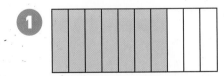   **2**

Find each missing numerator and denominator.

3 $\dfrac{1}{5} = \dfrac{\square}{10}$ **4**  $\dfrac{5}{10} = \dfrac{1}{\square}$ **5** 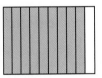 $\dfrac{4}{10} = \dfrac{2}{\square}$

Round to the nearest ten.

6 25   **7** 107

7.1 Understanding Tenths

Lesson Objectives

- Read and write tenths in decimal and fractional forms.
- Represent and interpret tenths models.

Vocabulary
tenth
decimal form
decimal point
expanded form

Learn Express fractions in tenths as decimals.

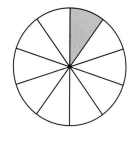 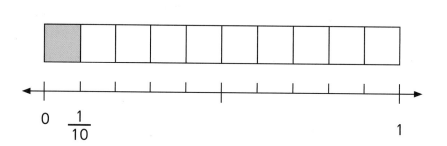

Each part is $\frac{1}{10}$ (one tenth).

Write $\frac{1}{10}$ as 0.1 in **decimal form**.

0.1 is 1 tenth written in decimal form.

0.1
↑
decimal point
Read 0.1 as one tenth.
Its value is 1 tenth.

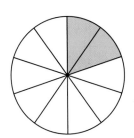

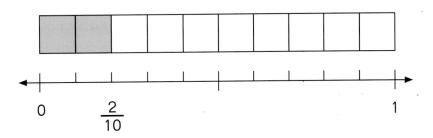

Two parts out of ten is $\frac{2}{10}$ (two tenths).

Write $\frac{2}{10}$ as 0.2 in decimal form.

In the same way, I can write $\frac{3}{10}$ as 0.3 and $\frac{4}{10}$ as 0.4.

Just like the fractions $\frac{1}{10}$ and $\frac{2}{10}$, 0.1 and 0.2 are parts of a whole.

0.1 and 0.2 are called decimals.

A decimal is a number with a decimal point, and digits to the right of the decimal point.

Guided Practice

Express each of these as a decimal.

1 $\frac{5}{10}$ =

2 $\frac{6}{10}$ =

3 3 tenths =

4 eight tenths =

Find the decimals that the shaded and unshaded parts represent.

5  shaded parts:

unshaded parts:

6 shaded parts:

unshaded parts:

Find the decimal for each point on the number line.

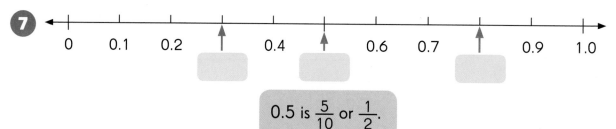

7

0   0.1   0.2   0.4   0.6   0.7   0.9   1.0

0.5 is $\frac{5}{10}$ or $\frac{1}{2}$.

Learn Find equivalent ones and tenths.

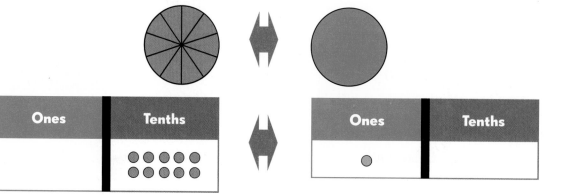

Ones	Tenths
	●●●●● ●●●●●

Ones	Tenths
●	

$\frac{10}{10}$ is equal to 1.

10 tenths = 1 one

You can regroup 10 tenths as 1 one.

Learn Express mixed numbers as decimals.

Rewrite $1\frac{6}{10}$ as a decimal.

Ones	Tenths
●	●●● ●●●
1	6

$1\frac{6}{10}$ = 1 one and 6 tenths

= 1.6

The word 'and' tells you where to put the decimal point. Read 1.6 as one and six tenths.

^{Learn} Express improper fractions as decimals.

Rewrite $\frac{12}{10}$ as a decimal.

Ones	Tenths

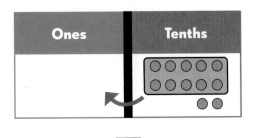

$$\frac{12}{10} = 12 \text{ tenths}$$

10 tenths = 1 one   2 tenths

$$\frac{12}{10} = 1 \text{ one and 2 tenths}$$
$$= 1.2$$

Ones	Tenths
○	○○
1	2

Decimals are another way of writing fractions and mixed numbers.

Guided Practice

Express each of these as a decimal.

8 15 tenths = ☐

9 2 ones and 3 tenths = ☐

Find the decimals that the shaded parts represent.

10 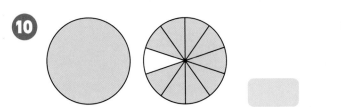 ☐

11 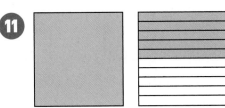 ☐

Look at the points marked ✗ on the number line.
Find the decimals that these points represent.

12

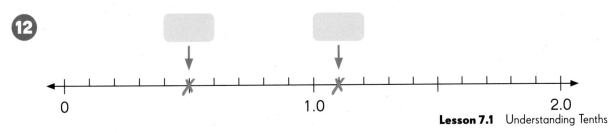

0   1.0   2.0

Express each of these as a decimal.

13

Ones	Tenths
● ●	● ● ● ● ● ●

[answer box]

14

Ones	Tenths
	● ● ● ● ● ● ● ● ● ● ● ● ● ● ● ● ● ●

[answer box]

15 $2\frac{9}{10}$ = [answer box]

16 $\frac{27}{10}$ = [answer box]

Express the length of each insect as a fraction and a decimal.

Example

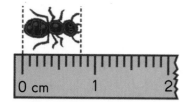

Length of ant $= \frac{8}{10}$ cm

$= 0.8$ cm

17

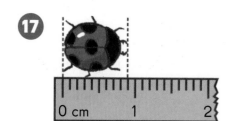

Length of ladybug $= \dfrac{\boxed{}}{10}$ cm

$=$ [answer box] cm

18

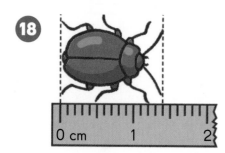

Length of beetle $=$ [answer box] cm

$=$ [answer box] cm

Express the total amount of water as a mixed number and a decimal.

19

Total amount of water = 1 $\dfrac{\boxed{}}{\boxed{}}$ L

= $\boxed{}$ L

Express each decimal as tenths.

20 0.9 = $\boxed{}$ tenths

21 0.7 = $\boxed{}$ tenths

22 1.1 = $\boxed{}$ tenths

23 4.3 = $\boxed{}$ tenths

Learn Write decimals to show their place values.

Tens	Ones	Tenths
4	2	3

42.3 = 4 tens + 2 ones + 3 tenths
= 40 + 2 + 0.3
= 40 + 2 + $\dfrac{3}{10}$

$40 + 2 + \dfrac{3}{10}$ is called the **expanded form** of a decimal.

Guided Practice

Find the missing numbers in expanded form.

24 76.4 = $\boxed{}$ tens + $\boxed{}$ ones + $\boxed{}$ tenths

= 70 + 6 + $\boxed{}$

= 70 + 6 + $\dfrac{\boxed{}}{10}$

Use place value to understand whole number and decimal amounts.

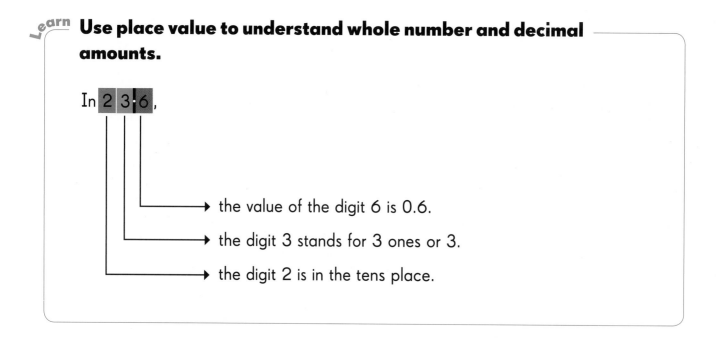

In 2 3.6 ,

→ the value of the digit 6 is 0.6.

→ the digit 3 stands for 3 ones or 3.

→ the digit 2 is in the tens place.

Guided Practice

Find the missing numbers.

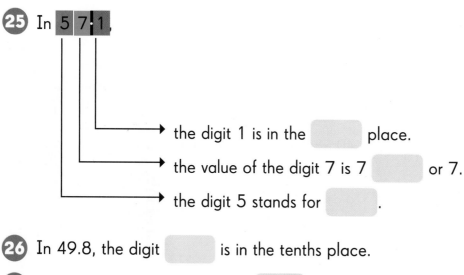

25 In 5 7.1 ,

→ the digit 1 is in the [   ] place.

→ the value of the digit 7 is 7 [   ] or 7.

→ the digit 5 stands for [   ].

26 In 49.8, the digit [   ] is in the tenths place.

27 In 95.6, the digit 5 stands for [   ].

28 In 50.2, the value of the digit 0 is [   ].

29 In 92.9, the two digits 9 stand for [   ] and [   ].

Let's Practice

Find the decimals that the shaded parts represent.

1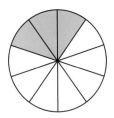

$$\frac{\boxed{}}{10} = \boxed{}$$

2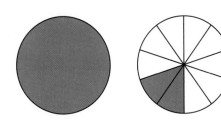

$$1\frac{\boxed{}}{10} = \boxed{}$$

Copy the number line. Mark ✗ to show where each decimal is located.

3 0.7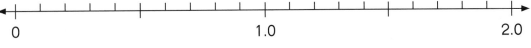

0   1.0   2.0

4 1.1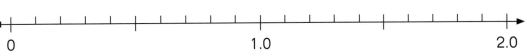

0   1.0   2.0

Express each of these as a decimal.

5

Ones	Tenths
● ●	● ● ● ● ●
	● ●

$$\boxed{}$$

6

Ones	Tenths
	● ● ● ● ●
	● ● ● ● ●
	● ● ● ●

$$\boxed{}$$

7 $\frac{4}{10}$ m = $\boxed{}$ m

8 7 tenths = $\boxed{}$

9 $\frac{16}{10}$ L = $\boxed{}$ L

10 14 tenths = $\boxed{}$

11 $2\frac{9}{10}$ kg = $\boxed{}$ kg

12 9 ones and 6 tenths = $\boxed{}$

Express each decimal as tenths.

13 0.3 = ☐ tenths

14 2.9 = ☐ tenths

Find the missing numbers.

15 3.5 = 3 ones and ☐ tenths

16 18.7 = ☐ ten 8 ones and ☐ tenths

17 7.5 = 7 + ☐

18 10.8 = ☐ + 0.8

19 $3.6 = 3 + \dfrac{6}{\boxed{}}$

20 $21.4 = \boxed{} + \boxed{} + \dfrac{\boxed{}}{10}$

Find the missing words or numbers.

Tens	Ones	Tenths
3	7	5

21 The digit 7 is in the ☐ place.

22 The digit 3 stands for ☐ .

23 The value of the digit 5 is ☐ .

ON YOUR OWN

Go to Workbook B:
Practice 1, pages 1–4

Lesson 7.2 Understanding Hundredths

Lesson Objectives

- Read and write hundredths in decimal and fractional forms.
- Represent and interpret hundredths models.

Vocabulary
hundredth

placeholder zero

Learn **Express fractions in hundredths as decimals.**

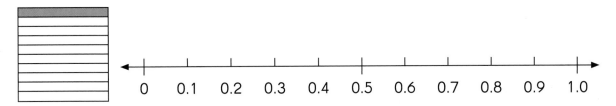

The square and the number line are each divided into 10 parts.
Each part is 1 tenth.

Divide each tenth into 10 parts.
Now the square and number line each have 100 equal parts.

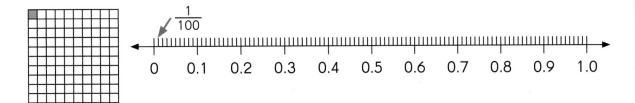

Each part is $\frac{1}{100}$ (one hundredth).

Write $\frac{1}{100}$ as 0.01 in decimal form.

$0.01 = \frac{1}{100}$
Read 0.01 as one hundredth.
Its value is 1 hundredth.

In the same way, write $\frac{2}{100}$ as 0.02 and $\frac{3}{100}$ as 0.03.

Guided Practice

Express each of these as a decimal.

1 $\frac{4}{100}$ oz = [ ] oz

2 $\frac{6}{100}$ in. = [ ] in.

3 five hundredths = [ ]

4 8 hundredths = [ ]

Find the decimals that the shaded parts represent.

5 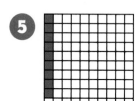 [ ]

6 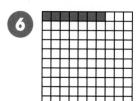 [ ]

Find the decimal for each point on the number line.

7

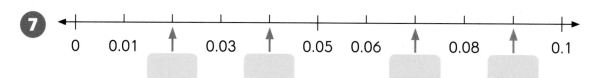

0   0.01   [ ]   0.03   [ ]   0.05   0.06   [ ]   0.08   [ ]   0.1

Learn Find equivalent tenths and hundredths.

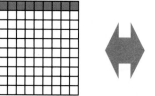

$\frac{10}{100}$ is equal to $\frac{1}{10}$ or 0.1.

10 hundredths = 1 tenth

You can regroup 10 hundredths as 1 tenth.

Express tenths and hundredths as decimals.

What is 2 tenths 5 hundredths written as a decimal?

Ones	Tenths	Hundredths
	●●	●●● ●●
0	2	5

2 tenths + 5 hundredths = 0.25

0.25 is twenty-five hundredths.

Express fractions as decimals.

Rewrite $\frac{15}{100}$ as a decimal.

$$\frac{15}{100} = 15 \text{ hundredths}$$

10 hundredths = 1 tenth

5 hundredths

Ones	Tenths	Hundredths
		○○○○○ ○○○○○ ●●●●●

Ones	Tenths	Hundredths
	●	●●●●●
0	1	5

$\frac{15}{100}$ = 1 tenth + 5 hundredths

= 0.1 + 0.05

= 0.15

Guided Practice

Express each of these as a decimal.

8 14 hundredths =

9 3 tenths 2 hundredths =

Find the decimals that the shaded parts represent.

10

11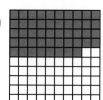

Look at the points marked X on the number line.
Find the decimals that these points represent.

12

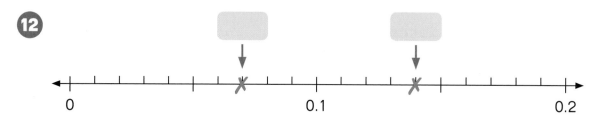

Express each of these as a decimal.

13

Ones	Tenths	Hundredths
	● ● ● ● ●	● ● ● ●

14

Ones	Tenths	Hundredths
		● ● ● ● ● ● ● ● ● ● ● ●

A tenth of a tenth is a hundredth.

15 $\frac{21}{100}$ =

16 $\frac{87}{100}$ =

Learn — Decimals can have placeholder zeros.

Does 0.90 have the same value as 0.9?

$0.90 = \dfrac{90}{100}$

$ = \dfrac{9}{10}$

$ = 0.9$

$\dfrac{90}{100} = \dfrac{9}{10}$ ($\div 10$ / $\div 10$)

Learn — Express ones, tenths, and hundredths as decimals.

What is 2 ones and 4 tenths 7 hundredths written as a decimal?

Ones	Tenths	Hundredths
● ●	● ● ● ●	● ● ● ● ● ● ●

2 ones and 4 tenths 7 hundredths
= 2 ones and 47 hundredths
= 2.47

Guided Practice

Express each of these as a decimal.

17

Ones	Tenths	Hundredths
● ● ●	●	● ● ● ● ● ● ● ●

18 4 ones and 9 tenths 1 hundredth = ☐

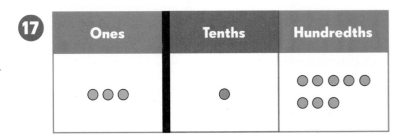

Find the decimal that the shaded parts represent.

 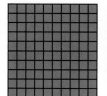 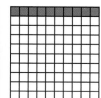

Look at the points marked X on the number line.
Find the decimals that these points represent.

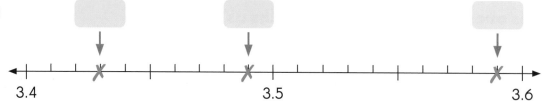

3.4   3.5   3.6

Learn **Express mixed numbers as decimals.**

Rewrite $1\frac{53}{100}$ as a decimal.

Ones	Tenths	Hundredths
○	○ ○ ○ ○ ○	○ ○ ○
1	5	3

$1\frac{53}{100}$ = 1 one and 5 tenths 3 hundredths
　　　 = 1 one and 53 hundredths
　　　 = 1.53

Learn **Express improper fractions as decimals.**

Rewrite $\frac{147}{100}$ as a decimal.

$\frac{147}{100}$ = 1 one and 47 hundredths
　　　 = 1.47

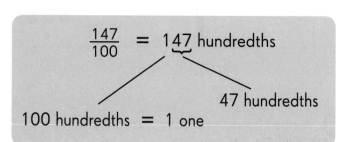

Guided Practice

Express each fraction or mixed number as a decimal.

21 $2\frac{75}{100} = \boxed{}$

22 $\frac{103}{100} = \boxed{}$

23 $3\frac{16}{100}$ L $= \boxed{}$ L

24 $\frac{204}{100}$ km $= \boxed{}$ km

Express each decimal as hundredths.

25 $0.03 = \boxed{}$ hundredths

26 $0.31 = \boxed{}$ hundredths

27 $6.17 = \boxed{}$ hundredths

28 $2.09 = \boxed{}$ hundredths

Le^{arn} Write decimals to show their place values.

Tens	Ones		Tenths	Hundredths
7	8	.	4	1

$78.41 = 7$ tens $+ 8$ ones $+ 4$ tenths $+ 1$ hundredth

$ = 70 + 8 + 0.4 + 0.01$

$ = 70 + 8 + \frac{4}{10} + \frac{1}{100}$

Guided Practice

Find the missing numbers in the expanded form.

29 $20.39 = \boxed{}$ tens $+ \boxed{}$ ones $+ \boxed{}$ tenths $+ \boxed{}$ hundredths

$ = 20 + 0.3 + \boxed{}$

$ = 20 + \dfrac{\boxed{}}{10} + \dfrac{\boxed{}}{100}$

^{Learn} Use place value to understand whole number and decimal amounts.

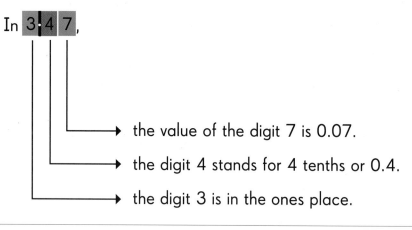

In 3.47,

→ the value of the digit 7 is 0.07.

→ the digit 4 stands for 4 tenths or 0.4.

→ the digit 3 is in the ones place.

Guided Practice

Find the missing words or numbers.

30 In 5.18, the digit 1 is in the [ ] place.

31 In 2.59, the value of the digit 9 is [ ].

32 In 82.03, the value of the digit 8 is [ ].

^{Learn} Use decimals to write dollars and cents.

One dollar → $1.00 = 100¢

17¢ = $0.17   70¢ = $0.70   7¢ = $0.07

Guided Practice

Express each amount using a dollar sign and decimal point.

33 53¢ = $ [   ]   **34** 30¢ = $ [   ]   **35** 3¢ = $ [   ]

Express each amount in decimal form.

Example
3 dollars and 25 cents = $3.25

A cent is $\frac{1}{100}$ of a dollar.

36 7 dollars and 40 cents = $ [   ]   **37** 18 dollars = $ [   ]

38 33 dollars and 5 cents = $ [   ]

Let's Practice

Find the decimals that the shaded parts represent.

1 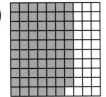 [   ]

2 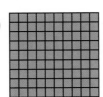 [   ]

**Look at the point marked X on each number line.
Find the decimals that these points represent.**

3

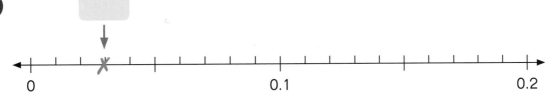

4

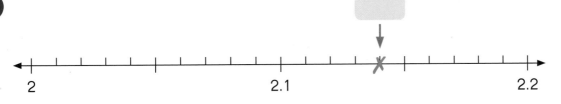

Copy each number line. Mark X to show where each decimal is located.

5 0.08

0   0.1   0.2

6 0.76
0.7   0.8   0.9

7 3.45

3.3   3.4   3.5

Express each of these as a decimal.

8

Ones	Tenths	Hundredths
	● ● ●	● ● ● ● ●

9

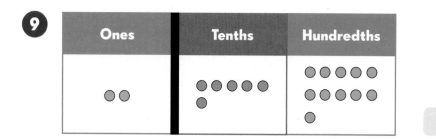

Ones	Tenths	Hundredths
● ●		

10 $\frac{35}{100}$ lb = _____ lb

11 3 L = _____ L

12 $\frac{308}{100}$ mi = _____ mi

13 $\frac{61}{100}$ = _____

14 2 tenths 9 hundredths = _____

15 8 ones and 4 hundredths = _____

Express each decimal as hundredths.

16 0.23 = _____ hundredths

17 4.01 = _____ hundredths

Find the missing numbers.

18 67.09 = ⬜ tens 7 ones and ⬜ hundredths

19 2.75 = 2 + 0.7 + ⬜

20 $7.25 = 7 + \dfrac{\square}{10} + \dfrac{5}{\square}$

Find the missing words or numbers.

Tens	Ones		Tenths	Hundredths
8	4	.	2	9

21 The digit 8 is in the ⬜ place.

22 The digit 2 stands for ⬜.

23 The value of the digit 9 is ⬜.

Express each amount using a dollar sign and decimal point.

24 35¢ = $⬜

25 50¢ = $⬜

26 9¢ = $⬜

Write each amount in decimal form.

27 9 dollars and 15 cents = $⬜

28 2 dollars and 40 cents = $⬜

29 24 dollars = $⬜

30 56 dollars and 5 cents = $⬜

ON YOUR OWN

Go to Workbook B:
Practice 2, pages 5–8

Lesson 7.3 Comparing Decimals

Lesson Objectives

- Compare and order decimals.
- Complete number patterns.

Learn **Use models to find 0.1 more than or 0.1 less than.**

What is 0.1 **more than** 0.6?

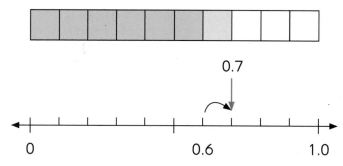

Each part is 0.1.

0.7 is 0.1 more than 0.6.

What is 0.1 **less than** 1.6?

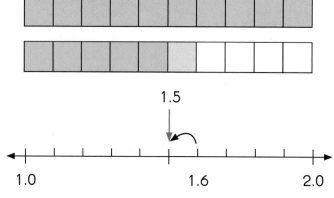

1.5 is 0.1 less than 1.6.

Learn   Find 0.01 more than or 0.01 less than.

What is 0.01 more than 0.22?

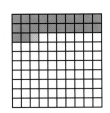 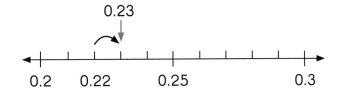

Each part is 0.01.
0.23 is 0.01 more than 0.22.

What is 0.01 less than 0.18?

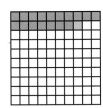 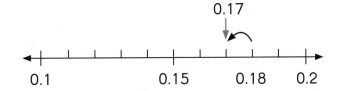

0.17 is 0.01 less than 0.18.

Guided Practice

Complete.

1 What number is 0.1 more than 1.2? ▭

2 What number is 0.1 less than 0.9? ▭

3 0.2 more than 8.7 is ▭ .

4 0.5 less than 4.9 is ▭ .

5 What number is 0.01 more than 0.15? ▭

6 What number is 0.01 less than 0.29? ▭

7 0.02 more than 6.24 is ▭ .

8 0.04 less than 7.16 is ▭ .

Learn

Find missing numbers in a pattern.

These decimals follow a pattern.
What are the next two decimals?

0.2   0.4   0.6   0.8   1.0 ...

1.2 is 0.2 more than 1.0.
1.4 is 0.2 more than 1.2.

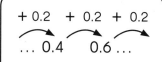

+ 0.2   + 0.2   + 0.2
... 0.4   0.6 ...
Add 0.2 to get
the next number.

The next two decimals are 1.2 and 1.4.

....

1.32   1.27   1.22   1.17   1.12

1.07 is 0.05 less than 1.12.
1.02 is 0.05 less than 1.07.

− 0.05   − 0.05   − 0.05
... 1.27   1.22 ...
Subtract 0.05 to get
the next number.

The next two decimals are 1.07 and 1.02.

Guided Practice

Find the missing numbers in each pattern.

9

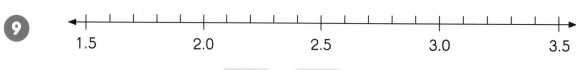

1.5   2.0   2.5   3.0   3.5

1.6   1.9   2.2   2.5   ☐   ☐

10

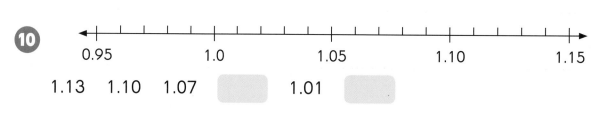

0.95   1.0   1.05   1.10   1.15

1.13   1.10   1.07   ☐   1.01   ☐

Let's Practice

Copy the number line. Find each decimal.
Then mark X to show where each decimal is located.

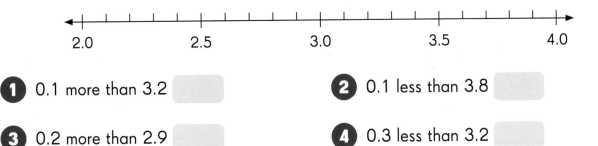

1 0.1 more than 3.2 ◻   **2** 0.1 less than 3.8 ◻

3 0.2 more than 2.9 ◻   **4** 0.3 less than 3.2 ◻

Copy the number line. Find each decimal.
Then mark X to show where each decimal is located.

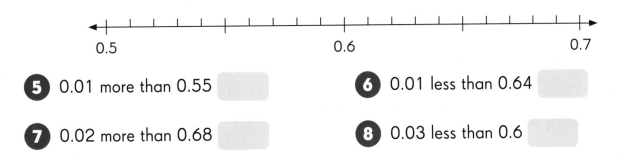

5 0.01 more than 0.55 ◻   **6** 0.01 less than 0.64 ◻

7 0.02 more than 0.68 ◻   **8** 0.03 less than 0.6 ◻

Find the missing numbers.

	Number	0.1 More Than the Number	0.01 More Than the Number
9	0.19		
10	1.73		
11	3.9		

Find the missing numbers.

	Number	0.1 Less Than the Number	0.01 Less Than the Number
12	0.28		
13	3.60		
14	7.1		

Find the missing numbers in each pattern.

15 2.2   2.4   2.6   [ ]   [ ]

16 3.34   3.37   [ ]   [ ]   3.46

17 6.23   [ ]   6.19   6.17   [ ]

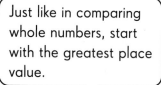

ON YOUR OWN

**Go to Workbook B:
Practice 3, pages 9–10**

Learn   Use place value concepts to compare decimals.

Which is greater, 0.4 or 0.34?

Ones		Tenths	Hundredths
0	.	4	
0	.	3	4

First, compare the ones. They are the same.
Next, compare the tenths.
4 tenths is **greater than** 3 tenths.
So, 0.4 is greater than 0.34 and
0.34 is less than 0.4.

greater than: >
less than: <

Just like in comparing whole numbers, start with the greatest place value.

Use place value concepts to order decimals.

Order 0.62, 0.23, and 0.6 from **least** to **greatest**.

Ones		Tenths	Hundredths
0		6	2
0		2	3
0		6	0

Remember
0.6 = 0.60.

First, compare the ones. They are the same.
Next, compare the tenths. 6 tenths is greater than 2 tenths.
So, 0.23 is the least.

Because 0.62 and 0.6 have the same tenths digits, compare the hundredths.
2 hundredths is greater than 0 hundredths.
So, 0.62 is greater than 0.6.
The order from least to greatest is 0.23, 0.6, 0.62.

Guided Practice

Compare. Use > or <.

11 0.76 ◯ 0.8

12 0.4 ◯ 0.24

13 0.21 ◯ 0.12

14 0.30 ◯ 0.33

Order the decimals from least to greatest.

15 0.18, 0.2, 0.15

16 0.8, 0.17, 0.31

17 1.04, 0.04, 0.14

18 0.20, 2.02, 0.22

You can use place-value charts to help you compare these decimals.

Game

Materials:
• 12 cards

Decimal Game!

STEP 1 Make a set of cards like these:

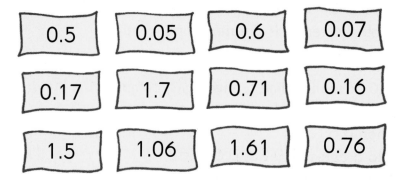

0.5	0.05	0.6	0.07
0.17	1.7	0.71	0.16
1.5	1.06	1.61	0.76

STEP 2 Shuffle the cards.

STEP 3 Draw three cards and order the decimals from least to greatest.

STEP 4 Your partner checks the answer.

STEP 5 Return the cards to the deck and shuffle them.

STEP 6 Take turns to order the decimals and check the answer.
Play three rounds each.

The player with the most correct answers wins!

 **Hands-On Activity**

WORKING TOGETHER

Work in groups of three.

STEP 1 Player 1 rolls the die twice to get a 2-digit decimal.
Do not use 0.01 and 0.99.

STEP 2 Player 2 says a decimal between 0 and 1 that is greater than
Player 1's decimal.

STEP 3 Player 3 says a decimal between 0 and 1 that is less than
Player 1's decimal.

STEP 4 Take turns forming a decimal between 0 and 1.
During each round, discuss your answers.

 Let's Explore!

WORK IN PAIRS

Your teacher will call out a decimal, such as 2.8.

STEP 1 Write this number on a place-value chart.

STEP 2 Insert a zero at any place in this decimal, for example, 2.08.
Write this number beneath the first one on the place-value chart.

STEP 3 Compare the decimal formed with the given decimal.
Then say whether it is greater than, less than, or equal to
the given decimal.

Example

2.08 is less than 2.8.

Ones		Tenths	Hundredths
2	.	8	
2	.	0	8

STEP 4 Next, insert the zero in a different place, and write
the number on your place-value chart.
For example, make 2.80.
Then say whether it is greater than, less than,
or equal to the given decimal.

Discuss with your classmates how inserting a zero in
the different places of a decimal will change its value.

Both Andy and Rita think that 0.23 is greater than 0.3.

23 is greater than 3,
so 0.23 is greater than 0.3.

23 tenths is greater
than 3 tenths, so 0.23
is greater than 0.3.

Do you agree? Why or why not? Explain your answer.

Let's Practice

Compare each pair of decimals. Use > or <.

1

Ones		Tenths	Hundredths
0	•	7	0
2	•	7	7

0.70 ⬤ 2.77

2

Ones		Tenths	Hundredths
2	•	7	6
2	•	7	7

2.76 ⬤ 2.77

Order the decimals from least to greatest.

3   0.49, 0.4, 0.53

4   2.8, 2.08, 2.88

Order the decimals from greatest to least.

5   0.51, 0.57, 1.02

6   4.32, 2.43, 3.24

ON YOUR OWN

**Go to Workbook B:
Practice 4, pages 11–12**

Lesson 7.4 Rounding Decimals

Lesson Objective

- Round decimals to the nearest whole number or tenth.

Vocabulary
round

Learn **Round decimals to the nearest whole number.**

The crack in the Liberty Bell is about 24.5 inches long.
Round 24.5 inches to the nearest inch.

24.0 ← round down | 24.5 | round up → 25.0

Look at 24.5 on the number line.
It is halfway between 24 and 25.
To round to the nearest whole number, look at the tenths digit.
Since it is 5, round up.
So, 24.5 rounded to the nearest whole number is 25.
The length of the crack in the Liberty Bell to the nearest inch is 25 inches.

Jasmine's mass is 35.2 kilograms.

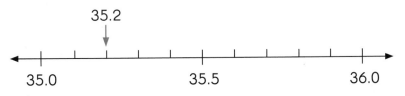

35.2

35.0   35.5   36.0

What is my mass to the nearest kilogram?

The number 35.2 is between 35 and 36.
It is nearer to 35 than to 36.
Since the tenths digit is less than 5, round down.
So, 35.2 rounded to the nearest whole number is 35.
Jasmine's mass to the nearest kilogram is 35 kilograms.

Continued on next page

Round 26.8 to the nearest whole number.

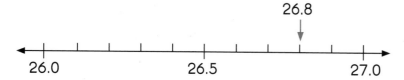

The number 26.8 is between 26 and 27.
It is nearer to 27 than to 26.
Since the tenths digit is greater than 5, round up.
So, 26.8 rounded to the nearest whole number is 27.

Round 14.68 to the nearest whole number.

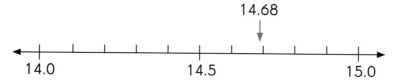

The number 14.68 is between 14 and 15.
It is nearer to 15 than to 14.
Since the tenths digit is greater than 5, round up.
So, 14.68 rounded to the nearest whole number is 15.

Round 39.45 to the nearest whole number.

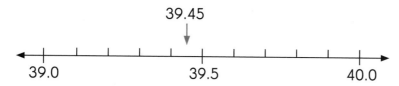

The number 39.45 is between 39 and 40.
It is nearer to 39 than to 40.
Since the tenths digit is less than 5, round down.
So, 39.45 rounded to the nearest whole number is 39.

What would 39.55 be, rounded to the nearest whole number?

Guided Practice

For each decimal, draw a number line. Mark X to show where the decimal is located. Then round it to the nearest whole number.

Example

5.8

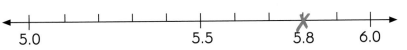

5.8 rounded to the nearest whole number is 6.

1 0.7   **2** 4.3   **3** 0.45   **4** 12.53

Let's Practice

Round the decimals to the nearest whole number.

1 Round 3.7 to the nearest whole number.

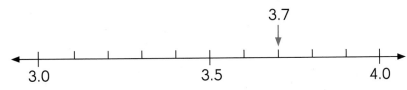

3.7 is between 3 and [ ].

3.7 is nearer to [ ] than to [ ].

3.7 rounded to the nearest whole number is [ ].

2 Round 1.84 to the nearest whole number.

1.84 is between 1 and [ ].

1.84 is nearer to [ ] than to [ ].

1.84 rounded to the nearest whole number is [ ].

ON YOUR OWN

Go to Workbook B:
Practice 5, pages 13–14

^{arn} **Round decimals to the nearest tenth.**

Dion's height is 0.83 meter. Round 0.83 meter to the nearest tenth of a meter.

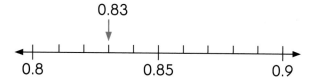

0.83 = 8 tenths 3 hundredths
0.83 is between 8 tenths (0.8) and 9 tenths (0.9).
It is nearer to 0.8 than to 0.9.
To round to the nearest tenth, look at the hundredths digit.
Since it is less than 5, round down.
So, 0.83 meter rounded to the nearest tenth is 0.8 meter.

Round 1.75 to the nearest tenth.

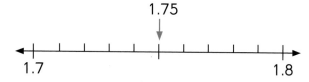

1.75 is halfway between 1.7 and 1.8.
Since the hundredths digit is 5, round up.
So, 1.75 rounded to the nearest tenth is 1.8.

Round 2.98 to the nearest tenth.

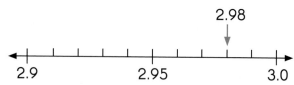

2.98 is between 2.9 and 3.
It is nearer to 3 than to 2.9.
Since the hundredths digit is greater than 5, round up.
So, 2.98 rounded to the nearest tenth is 3.0.
3 is written as 3.0 to one decimal place.

Guided Practice

For each decimal, draw a number line. Mark ✗ to show where the decimal is located. Then round it to the nearest tenth.

Example

3.43

So, 3.43 rounded to the nearest tenth is 3.4.

5 0.36 ____   **6** 2.32 ____   **7** 4.05 ____

 **Hands-On Activity**

Material:
• measuring tape

 **WORKING TOGETHER**

Work in groups of four or five.

STEP 1 Place the measuring tape on the floor, metric side up.

STEP 2 Each member should take turns to walk 5 steps beside the measuring tape.

STEP 3 Measure the distance in meters to two decimal places.

STEP 4 Record the readings in a table.

STEP 5 Round each distance to the nearest tenth of a meter.

Example

Name of Student	Distance (m)	
	Actual Reading	**Rounded Reading**
Eduardo	1.29	1.3

Let's Explore!

Example

A number has two decimal places.

It is 1.7 when rounded to the nearest tenth.

What could the number be?

Zach draws a number line to find the number.

1.64 **1.65** **1.66** **1.67** **1.68** **1.69** 1.70 **1.71** **1.72** **1.73** **1.74** 1.75

The numbers in **green** are the possible answers.

A number has two decimal places.
It is 4.2 when rounded to one decimal place.

1   What could the number be? List the possible answers.

2   Which of these numbers is the greatest?

3   Which of these numbers is the least?

Let's Practice

Find the missing numbers.

1 Round 0.24 to the nearest tenth.

0.24

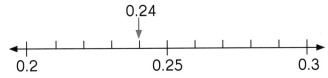

0.2				0.25				0.3		

0.24 is between [ ] and [ ] .

0.24 is nearer to [ ] than to [ ] .

0.24 rounded to the nearest tenth is [ ] .

2 Round 5.17 to the nearest tenth.

5.17 is between [ ] and 5.2.

5.17 is nearer to [ ] than to [ ] .

5.17 rounded to the nearest tenth is [ ] .

3 Round each decimal to the nearest whole number and the nearest tenth.

Decimal	Rounded to the Nearest	
	Whole Number	Tenth
3.49	[ ]	[ ]
4.85	[ ]	[ ]

ON YOUR OWN

**Go to Workbook B:
Practice 6, pages 15–16**

Lesson 7.5 Fractions and Decimals

Lesson Objective

- Express a fraction as a decimal and a decimal as a fraction.

Vocabulary
equivalent fraction

Learn Express fractions as decimals.

Express the fraction $\frac{1}{5}$ as a decimal.

Look at the bar model and the number line.

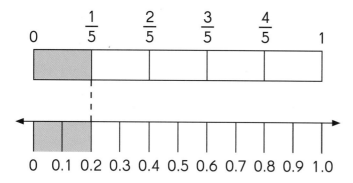

So, $\frac{1}{5}$ is 0.2 as a decimal.

Here is another way to show that $\frac{1}{5} = 0.2$.

$$\frac{1}{5} \overset{\times 2}{=} \frac{2}{10} = 0.2$$
$$\underset{\times 2}{}$$

Find an **equivalent fraction** with a denominator of 10 or 100.

Fractions show a whole divided into any number of parts. Decimals show a whole divided into 10 or 100 parts.

To express a fraction as a decimal, find an equivalent fraction with a denominator that is 10 or 100.

Guided Practice

Complete.

1

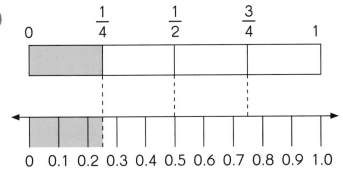

0      $\frac{1}{4}$ $\frac{1}{2}$ $\frac{3}{4}$ 1

0 0.1 0.2 0.3 0.4 0.5 0.6 0.7 0.8 0.9 1.0

From the bar model and number line, you can see that

$\frac{1}{4}$ = 0.25.

You can also see that

$\frac{1}{2}$ = [   ] and $\frac{3}{4}$ = [   ].

2 Express $\frac{1}{4}$ as a decimal.

$$\frac{1}{4} \xrightarrow{\times 25} \frac{25}{100} = 0.25$$

Can you find an equivalent fraction of $\frac{1}{4}$ with a denominator of 10?

No. But I can find an equivalent fraction with a denominator of 100.

So, $\frac{1}{4}$ is [   ] in decimal form.

Learn Express an improper fraction as a decimal.

Express $\frac{5}{4}$ as a decimal.

$\frac{5}{4} = \frac{4}{4} + \frac{1}{4}$

    $= 1 + \frac{1}{4}$

    $= 1 + 0.25$

    $= 1.25$

$\frac{1}{4} = 0.25$

Guided Practice

Complete.

3 Express $\frac{8}{5}$ as a decimal.

$$\frac{8}{5} = \frac{5}{5} + \frac{\boxed{}}{5}$$

$$= 1 + \boxed{}$$

$$= \boxed{}$$

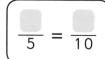

$$\frac{\boxed{}}{5} = \frac{\boxed{}}{10}$$

Express each fraction as a decimal.

4 $\frac{2}{5}$ $\boxed{}$

5 $\frac{9}{20}$ $\boxed{}$

6 $\frac{5}{2}$ $\boxed{}$

Learn **Express mixed numbers as decimals.**

Express $3\frac{1}{2}$ as a decimal.

Method 1

$$3\frac{1}{2} = \frac{7}{2}$$

$$= \frac{7 \times 5}{2 \times 5}$$

$$= \frac{35}{10}$$

$$= 3.5$$

Method 2

$$\frac{1}{2} = \frac{5}{10}$$

$$= 0.5$$

$$3\frac{1}{2} = 3 + \frac{1}{2}$$

$$= 3 + 0.5$$

$$= 3.5$$

The whole number 3 remains unchanged. Rewrite the fraction $\frac{1}{2}$ as a decimal.

So, $3\frac{1}{2}$ is 3.5 in decimal form.

Guided Practice

Express each mixed number as a decimal.

7 $2\frac{3}{5}$ $\boxed{}$

8 $9\frac{1}{4}$ $\boxed{}$

9 $5\frac{27}{50}$ $\boxed{}$

^{Learn} Express decimals as fractions.

Express 0.8 as a fraction in simplest form.

0   0.1   0.2   0.3   0.4   0.5   0.6   0.7   0.8   0.9   1.0

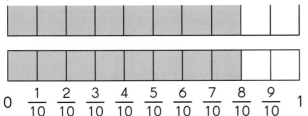

$0 \quad \frac{1}{10} \quad \frac{2}{10} \quad \frac{3}{10} \quad \frac{4}{10} \quad \frac{5}{10} \quad \frac{6}{10} \quad \frac{7}{10} \quad \frac{8}{10} \quad \frac{9}{10} \quad 1$

$0.8 = \frac{8}{10}$

$\quad\ \ = \frac{4}{5}$

Divide the numerator and denominator of $\frac{8}{10}$ by 2.

$\frac{8}{10} = \frac{4}{5}$

^{Learn} Express decimals as mixed numbers.

Express 2.5 as a mixed number in simplest form.

$2.5 = \frac{25}{10}$

$\quad\ \ = \frac{20}{10} + \frac{5}{10}$

$\quad\ \ = 2 + \frac{1}{2}$

$\quad\ \ = 2\frac{1}{2}$

Divide the numerator and denominator of $\frac{5}{10}$ by 5.

Express 7.25 as a mixed number in simplest form.

$7.25 = 7 + 0.25$

$\quad\ \ = 7 + \frac{25}{100}$

$\quad\ \ = 7 + \frac{1}{4}$

$\quad\ \ = 7\frac{1}{4}$

$\frac{25}{100} = \frac{5}{20} = \frac{1}{4}$

Guided Practice

Express each decimal as a fraction or a mixed number in simplest form.

10 0.4

11 3.75

12 2.45

Players: **4** or **5**
Materials:
• decimal cards
• fraction cards

Match Game

STEP 1 Put all the decimal cards face up on a table.

STEP 2 Shuffle the fraction cards. Then turn over the fraction card at the top of the stack.

STEP 3 Check if the fraction on the card shown is equivalent to any of the decimal cards on the table.

> **Example**
> The fraction $\frac{1}{5}$ is equivalent to the decimal 0.2.

STEP 4 The fastest player to find a match will say 'Decimal snap!' and collect the two cards.

STEP 5 The other players check the answer. If the answer is wrong, the cards are taken away from the player. The fraction card is put back at the bottom of the stack of fraction cards, and the decimal card is returned to the table.

STEP 6 Turn over the next fraction card to continue the game.

Play until no more matches can be found.

The player who collects the most matching cards wins!

Draw a bar model and a number line.
Find the missing numbers.

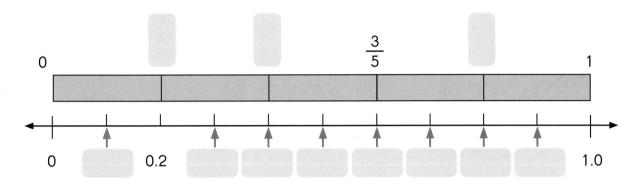

Use the bar model and number line to express each fraction
as a decimal.

1 $\frac{1}{5}$

2 $\frac{3}{5}$

3 $\frac{4}{5}$

Express each fraction as a decimal.

4 $\frac{3}{4}$

5 $\frac{17}{20}$

6 $\frac{26}{25}$

Express each mixed number as a decimal.

7 $3\frac{13}{50}$

8 $7\frac{24}{25}$

9 $22\frac{4}{5}$

Express each decimal as a fraction or a mixed number in simplest form.

10 0.2

11 0.75

12 0.28

13 3.6

14 5.12

15 4.35

ON YOUR OWN

Go to Workbook B:
Practice 7, pages 17–18

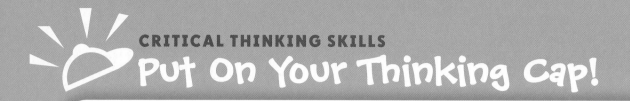
PROBLEM SOLVING

Suppose this paper strip is 1 unit long. Trace and cut out the paper strip. Use your paper strip to measure these line segments to the nearest tenth of a unit.

Example
The line segment is about 0.7 unit.

1

2

3

4

How can you check whether your measurement is accurate?

Put On Your Thinking Cap!

PROBLEM SOLVING

Suppose this paper strip is 1 unit long. Trace and cut out the paper strip. Use your paper strip to measure these line segments to the nearest hundredth of a unit.

Example

The line segment is about 0.65 unit.

How many tenths are in the paper strip?
How many hundredths are in 1 tenth?

5

6

7

8

ON YOUR OWN

**Go to Workbook B:
Put on Your Thinking Cap!
pages 19–20**

Chapter Wrap Up

Study Guide

You have learned...

BIG IDEAS
▶ Decimals are another way to show amounts that are parts of a whole.
▶ A decimal has a decimal point to the right of the ones place and digits to the right of the decimal point.

Decimals

Read, Write, and Express in Expanded Form

2.53

- 2 ones and 5 tenths 3 hundredths
- two and fifty-three hundredths
- $2.53 = 2 + 0.5 + 0.03$
- $2.53 = 2 + \frac{5}{10} + \frac{3}{100}$

Place Value

2.53

→ 3 hundredths
→ 5 tenths
→ 2 ones

Patterns

- 1.2   1.3   1.4 ...
  The next number is 1.5.
- 2.28   2.26   2.24 ...
  The next number is 2.22.

Compare and Order

3.4   3.64   3.46

- $3.46 < 3.64$
- $3.46 > 3.4$
- 3.4 is the least number.
- 3.64 is the greatest number.
- The numbers in order from least to greatest are 3.4, 3.46, 3.64.

Round to

- the nearest whole number: 3.6 is about 4.
- the nearest tenth: 3.62 is about 3.6.

Fractions and Decimals

- $\frac{9}{10} = 0.9$, $\frac{3}{4} = \frac{75}{100}$
  $= 0.75$
- $3.4 = 3\frac{4}{10}$
  $= 3\frac{2}{5}$

Chapter Review/Test

Vocabulary

Choose the correct word.

tenths	least
decimal point	greater than
decimal form	greatest
hundredths	order
placeholder zero	round
more than	equivalent fraction
less than	expanded form

1 $\frac{3}{10}$ is written as 0.3 in _____ .

2 In the decimal 0.43, the digit 3 has a value of 3 _____ .

3 The decimal 0.44 has a value equal to 4 _____ 4 _____ .

Concepts and Skills

Express each fraction as a decimal.

4 $\frac{3}{10}$ _____

5 $\frac{23}{10}$ _____

6 $\frac{127}{100}$ _____

Express the value of each decimal in ones, tenths, and hundredths.

Example

2.73 = 2 ones and 7 tenths 3 hundredths

7 0.36 _____

8 3.07 _____

4.12 can be written as $4 + \frac{1}{10} + \frac{2}{100}$. Complete in the same way.

9 0.35 = _____ + _____

10 1.70 = _____ + _____

11 2.04 = _____ + _____

Continue the pattern.

12   0.2   0.5   0.8   1.1   **13**   4.56   4.54   4.52   4.50

Compare. Use > or <.

14   4.1   ⚪   4.11   **15**   3.02   ⚪   3.20

16   0.6   ⚪   0.59   **17**   5.87   ⚪   5.70

Order the decimals from greatest to least.

18   9.08   9.80   8.09   0.98

19   4.62   4.26   6.42   6.24

Round 9.75 to

20   the nearest whole number:

     the nearest tenth:

Express each fraction as a decimal.

21 $\frac{4}{5}$ **22** $\frac{1}{4}$ **23** $\frac{5}{2}$

Express each decimal as a fraction or mixed number in simplest form.

24   0.07   **25**   0.46   **26**   8.75

8 Adding and Subtracting Decimals

This is Mr. Romero's receipt from a supermarket.

SUPER SAVE MARKET

Item	Amount
Broccoli	$3.38
Lettuce	$2.98
Grapefruit	$0.99
Chicken	$6.87
Tomato	$3.18
Grapes	$4.47
Apples	$3.87
Total	$25.74
Cash Payment	$30.00
Change	$4.26

Thank you for shopping at Super Save Market.

Add to find the total. Subtract to find the amount of change.
$30.00 − $25.74 = $4.26
I received $4.26 change.

Lessons

8.1 Adding Decimals

8.2 Subtracting Decimals

8.3 Real-World Problems: Decimals

BIG IDEA

▶ Decimals can be added and subtracted in the same ways as whole numbers.

Recall Prior Knowledge

Regrouping ones

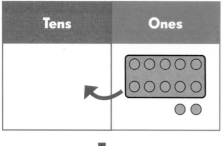

10 ones = 1 ten

12 ones = 1 ten 2 ones
       = 12

Regrouping tenths

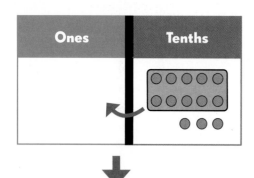

10 tenths = 1 one

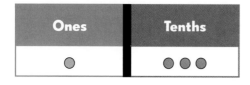

13 tenths = 1 one and 3 tenths
        = 1.3

Regrouping hundredths

Ones	Tenths	Hundredths

10 hundredths = 1 tenth

Ones	Tenths	Hundredths
	◯	◯◯◯◯
0	1	4

14 hundredths
= 1 tenth 4 hundredths
= 0.14

 Quick Check

Regroup.

1

Tens	Ones
	◯◯◯◯◯ ◯◯◯◯◯ ◯◯◯◯◯ ◯

16 ones = ⬜

2

Ones	Tenths
	◯◯◯◯◯ ◯◯◯◯◯ ◯◯◯◯◯ ◯◯◯◯

19 tenths = ⬜

3

Ones	Tenths	Hundredths
		◯◯◯◯◯ ◯◯◯◯ ◯◯◯◯ ◯◯

17 hundredths = ⬜

Lesson 8.1 Adding Decimals

Lesson Objective

- Add decimals up to two decimal places.

Learn **Add decimals with one decimal place without regrouping.**

Aisha hopped 0.4 meter from the starting line.
From there she hopped another 0.5 meter.
How far did she hop in all?

0.4 + 0.5 = ?

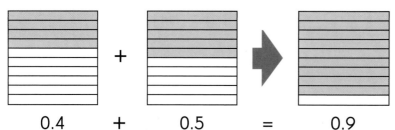

| 0.4 | + | 0.5 | = | 0.9 |

Each square represents 10 tenths or 1.

Write the numbers.
Line up the decimal points.
Add the tenths.

$$
\begin{array}{r}
0.\;4 \\
+\;\;0.\;5 \\
\hline
0.\;9
\end{array}
$$

Ones	Tenths
0.4	⦿⦿⦿⦿
0.5	⦿⦿⦿⦿⦿

4 tenths + 5 tenths = 9 tenths

Ones	Tenths
	⦿⦿⦿⦿⦿ ⦿⦿⦿⦿
0 •	9

A decimal in tenths has one decimal place.

So, 0.4 + 0.5 = 0.9.

She hopped 0.9 meter in all.

Learn Add decimals with one decimal place with regrouping in tenths.

Add 0.6 and 0.7.

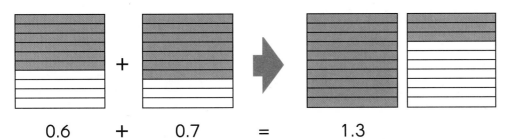

| 0.6 | + | 0.7 | = | 1.3 |

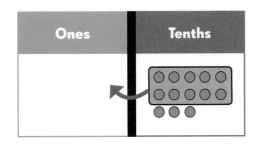

Write the numbers.
Line up the decimal points.
Add the tenths.

$$
\begin{array}{r}
\overset{1}{0}.\,6 \\
+\ \ 0.\,7 \\
\hline
1.\,3
\end{array}
$$

6 tenths + 7 tenths = 13 tenths

Regroup the tenths.

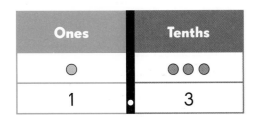

13 tenths = 10 tenths + 3 tenths

= 1 one and 3 tenths

So, 0.6 + 0.7 = 1.3.

Make Wholes

STEP
1 Player 1 puts his or her 🧊 into two groups.
Player 1 then counts the 🧊 and writes
two decimals with one decimal place.

Materials:
- 10 decimal squares
  per player
- some unit cubes
  per player

Example

0.6   +   0.5   =   ?

STEP
2 Player 2 adds the decimals by shading the decimal squares.

Example

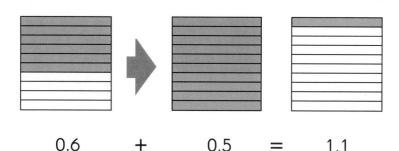

0.6   +   0.5   =   1.1

STEP
3 Player 2 gets 1 point for shading and saying aloud the answer correctly.

STEP
4 Take turns to play.

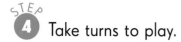

The player with more points after five rounds wins the game!

Learn Add decimals with one decimal place with regrouping in ones and tenths.

Add 5.4 and 7.8.

5.4

7.8

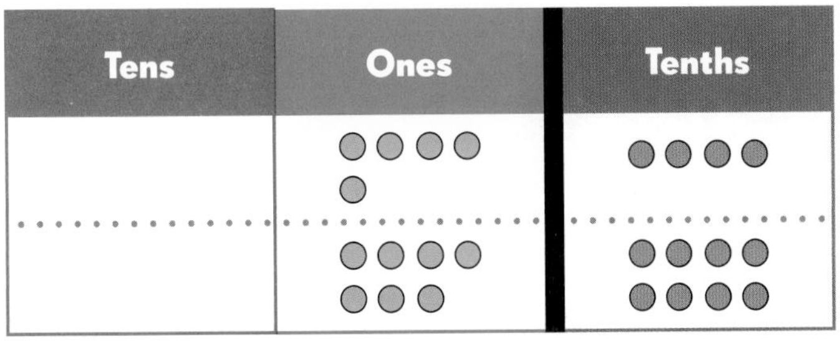
Tens
Ones
Tenths

Write the numbers.
Line up the decimal points.

Step 1
Add the tenths.

$$\begin{array}{r} \overset{1}{5}.\,4 \\ +\ 7.\,8 \\ \hline .\,2 \end{array}$$

4 tenths + 8 tenths
= 12 tenths
= 10 tenths + 2 tenths
= 1 one and 2 tenths

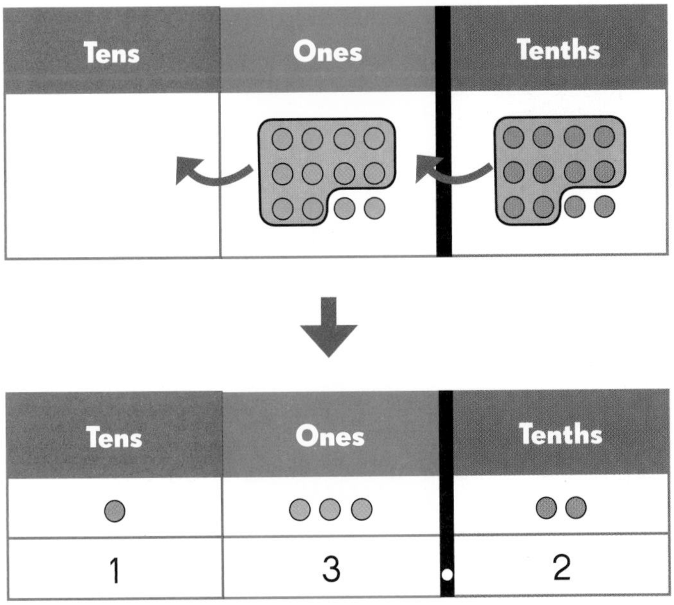
Tens
Ones
Tenths
Tens
Ones
Tenths
1
3
2

Step 2
Add the ones.

$$\begin{array}{r} \overset{1}{5}.\,4 \\ +\ 7.\,8 \\ \hline 13.\,2 \end{array}$$

1 one + 5 ones + 7 ones
= 13 ones
= 10 ones + 3 ones
= 1 ten 3 ones

So, 5.4 + 7.8 = 13.2.

Guided Practice

Regroup.

1. 16 tenths = ____ one and ____ tenths

2. 3 tenths + 9 tenths = ____ tenths
= ____ one and ____ tenths

Add.

3
```
    0 . 4
+   0 . 2
```

4
```
    0 . 5
+   0 . 6
```

5
```
    3 . 5
+   2 . 9
```

Copy and write in vertical form. Then add.

6 2.3 + 3.5

7 5.9 + 8

8 7.6 + 4.8

Let's Practice

Add.

1
```
    0 . 3
+   0 . 4
```

2
```
    4 . 5
+   3 . 2
```

Complete.

3 18 tenths = [ ] one and [ ] tenths

4 6 tenths + 8 tenths = [ ] tenths

= [ ] one and [ ] tenths

5
```
    2 . 4
+   4 . 6
```

6
```
    5 . 8
+   1 . 4
```

Copy and write in vertical form. Then add.

7 2.6 + 0.7

8 1.8 + 2.8

ON YOUR OWN

**Go to Workbook B:
Practice 1, pages 21–22**

Learn **Add decimals with two decimal places without regrouping.**

Kelvin has 2 pennies. Jasmine has 7 pennies.
How much money do they have altogether?

2 pennies is $0.02.
7 pennies is $0.07.

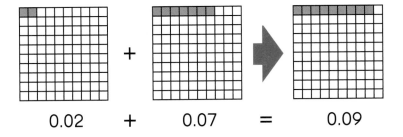

$$0.02 \quad + \quad 0.07 \quad = \quad 0.09$$

	Ones	Tenths	Hundredths
0.02			●●
0.07			●●● ●●●

Write the numbers.
Line up the decimal points.

	Ones	Tenths	Hundredths
			●●●● ●●●● ●
	0	0	9

Add the hundredths.

$$
\begin{array}{r}
0.0\,2 \\
+\ 0.0\,7 \\
\hline
0.0\,9
\end{array}
$$

2 hundredths + 7 hundredths
= 9 hundredths

So, $0.02 + $0.07 = $0.09.

They have $0.09 altogether.

A decimal with hundredths has two decimal places.

Add decimals with two decimal places with regrouping in hundredths.

Add 0.08 and 0.26.

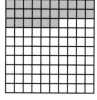 + →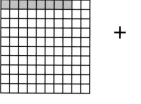

0.08　　　　+　　　0.26　　　=　　　0.34

	Ones	Tenths	Hundredths
0.08			●●●● ●●●●
0.26		●●	●●●● ●●

Write the numbers.
Line up the decimal points.

Step 1
Add the hundredths.

$$\begin{array}{r} 0.0\overset{1}{}8 \\ + \ 0.26 \\ \hline .4 \end{array}$$

	Ones	Tenths	Hundredths
		●●	⟨●●● ●●● ●●●⟩ ● ●●

8 hundredths + 6 hundredths

= 14 hundredths

Regroup the hundredths.

14 hundredths

= 10 hundredths +
　4 hundredths

= 1 tenth 4 hundredths

	Ones	Tenths	Hundredths
		●●●	●●●●
	0	3	4

Step 2
Add the tenths.

$$\begin{array}{r} 0.\overset{1}{0}8 \\ + \ 0.26 \\ \hline 0.34 \end{array}$$

1 tenth + 0 tenths + 2 tenths
= 3 tenths

So, 0.08 + 0.26 = 0.34.

Learn Add decimals with two decimal places with regrouping in tenths and hundredths.

Add 1.47 and 3.95.

> To add decimals, first write the numbers in vertical form. Make sure you line up the decimal points.

Step 1
Add the hundredths.

$$
\begin{array}{r}
1.4\overset{1}{7} \\
+\ 3.9\ 5 \\
\hline
2
\end{array}
$$

7 hundredths + 5 hundredths
= 12 hundredths
Regroup the hundredths.
12 hundredths
= 10 hundredths + 2 hundredths
= 1 tenth 2 hundredths

Step 2
Add the tenths.

$$
\begin{array}{r}
\overset{1}{1}.\overset{1}{4}\ 7 \\
+\ 3.9\ 5 \\
\hline
.4\ 2
\end{array}
$$

1 tenth + 4 tenths
+ 9 tenths = 14 tenths
Regroup the tenths.
14 tenths = 10 tenths
+ 4 tenths
= 1 one 4 tenths

Step 3
Add the ones.

$$
\begin{array}{r}
\overset{1}{1}.\overset{1}{4}\ 7 \\
+\ 3.9\ 5 \\
\hline
5.4\ 2
\end{array}
$$

1 one + 1 one
+ 3 ones
= 5 ones

So, 1.47 + 3.95 = 5.42.

Guided Practice

Complete.

9 13 hundredths = ⬚ tenth ⬚ hundredths

10 7 hundredths + 4 hundredths = ⬚ hundredths

= ⬚ tenth ⬚ hundredth

Add.

11
$$
\begin{array}{r}
0.0\ 8 \\
+\ 0.0\ 4 \\
\hline

\end{array}
$$

12
$$
\begin{array}{r}
0.1\ 8 \\
+\ 0.3\ 9 \\
\hline

\end{array}
$$

13
$$
\begin{array}{r}
3.4\ 6 \\
+\ 0.7\ 6 \\
\hline

\end{array}
$$

Copy and write in vertical form. Then add.

14 4.5 + 6.48 [ ]

15 $10.25 + $6.35 [ ]

16 $1.99 + $1.05 [ ]

Let's Practice

Add.

1
```
    0.06
  + 0.03
  ------
```
[ ]

2
```
    5.63
  + 2.25
  ------
```
[ ]

Regroup.

3 17 hundredths = [ ] tenth [ ] hundredths

4 7 hundredths + 6 hundredths = [ ] hundredths

= [ ] tenth [ ] hundredths

Add.

5
```
    0.38
  + 0.05
  ------
```
[ ]

6
```
    4.4
  + 1.99
  ------
```
[ ]

7
```
    2.49
  + 1.86
  ------
```
[ ]

Copy and write in vertical form. Then add.

8 8.4 + 3.67 [ ]

9 $13.58 + $0.69 [ ]

ON YOUR OWN

Go to Workbook B:
Practice 2, pages 23–26

Lesson Objective

- Subtract decimals up to two decimal places.

Learn **Subtract decimals with one decimal place without regrouping.**

A bottle has 0.5 liter of water. Abby drinks 0.3 liter of water from it.
How much water is left in the bottle?

0.5 – 0.3 = ?

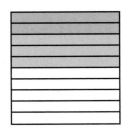

Ones	Tenths
	⊘ ⊘ ⊘ ◯ ◯

Take away
3 tenths.

Write the numbers.
Line up the decimal points.
Subtract the tenths.

$$\begin{array}{r} 0.5 \\ -\ 0.3 \\ \hline 0.2 \end{array}$$

5 tenths − 3 tenths = 2 tenths

So, 0.5 – 0.3 = 0.2.

0.2 liter of water is left in the bottle.

Guided Practice

Subtract.

1
```
   0 . 9
 − 0 . 1
```

2
```
   3 . 5
 − 1 . 4
```

3
```
   9 . 9
 − 0 . 9
```

Copy and write in vertical form. Then subtract.

4 8.9 − 7.8

5 7.3 − 4

6 9.7 − 2.1

---

^{Learn} **Subtract decimals with one decimal place with regrouping in ones and tenths.**

Subtract 0.7 from 1.5.

You cannot subtract 7 tenths from 5 tenths. Regroup 1 one and 5 tenths.

1.5

1 one and 5 tenths = 15 tenths

Write the numbers.
Line up the decimal points.
Subtract the tenths.

```
    0  1
    1 . 5
  − 0 . 7
    0 . 8
```

So, 1.5 − 0.7 = 0.8.

15 tenths − 7 tenths = 8 tenths

Guided Practice

Regroup.

7 1 = [ ] tenths

8 1.6 = [ ] tenths

9 6 = 5 ones and [ ] tenths

10 8.7 = 7 ones and [ ] tenths

Subtract.

11
```
   1 . 0
−  0 . 4
─────────
[        ]
```

12
```
   7 . 2
−  0 . 5
─────────
[        ]
```

Copy and write in vertical form. Then subtract.

13 3.5 − 2.7 [ ]

14 5.8 − 3.9 [ ]

Learn — Subtract decimals with one decimal place from whole numbers.

Subtract 0.8 from 2.
You can write 2 as 2.0.
Write the numbers. Line up the decimal points.

Step 1
Subtract the tenths.

```
  ¹ ¹
  2 . 0
− 0 . 8
───────
    . 2
```

Step 2
Subtract the ones.

```
  ¹ ¹
  2 . 0
− 0 . 8
───────
  1 . 2
```

You cannot subtract 8 tenths from 0 tenths.
Regroup 2 ones.
2 ones = 1 one and 10 tenths

So, 2.0 − 0.8 = 1.2.

Guided Practice

Copy and write in vertical form. Then subtract.

15 6 − 3.6 [ ]

16 11 − 3.2 [ ]

Break a Whole!

STEP 1 Each player starts with 1 ▭ .
It stands for 1 whole.

Materials:
• a ten-sided die
• unit cubes
• ten-rods

STEP 2 Player 1 rolls the ten-sided die.

STEP 3 Based on the number rolled, player 1 trades ▭ for

and takes away this number of ▪ from his or her ▭ .

Example

STEP 4 Player 1 counts the ▪ left and writes a subtraction sentence like this:
1 − 0.4 = 0.6.

STEP 5 Take turns to play.

....
The first player to take away all the ▪ wins the game!
....

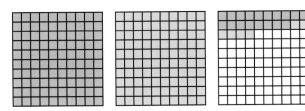

Subtract decimals with two decimal places with regrouping in tenths and hundredths.

Subtract 1.06 from 2.24.

You cannot subtract 6 hundredths from 4 hundredths.
Regroup 2 ones and 2 tenths 4 hundredths.

2 ones and 2 tenths $+$ 4 hundredths
$=$ 2 ones and 1 tenth $+$ 14 hundredths

Ones	Tenths	Hundredths
○ ○	●	● ● ● ●

Ones	Tenths	Hundredths
○ ⊘	●	● ● ● ● ● ● ● ⊘ ⊘ ⊘ ⊘ ⊘ ⊘

Write the numbers.
Line up the decimal points.

Step 1

Subtract the hundredths.

$$\begin{array}{r} 2.\overset{1}{\cancel{2}}\,{}^{1}4 \\ -\ 1.0\ 6 \\ \hline 8 \end{array}$$

14 hundredths $-$ 6 hundredths
$=$ 8 hundredths

Step 2

Subtract the tenths.

$$\begin{array}{r} 2.\overset{1}{\cancel{2}}\,{}^{1}4 \\ -\ 1.0\ 6 \\ \hline .1\ 8 \end{array}$$

1 tenth $-$ 0 tenths $=$ 1 tenth

Step 3

Subtract the ones.

$$\begin{array}{r} 2.\overset{1}{\cancel{2}}\,{}^{1}4 \\ -\ 1.0\ 6 \\ \hline 1.1\ 8 \end{array}$$

2 ones $-$ 1 one $=$ 1 one

So, 2.24 $-$ 1.06 $=$ 1.18.

Guided Practice

Regroup.

17 $0.35 = 2$ tenths ▢ hundredths

18 $1.26 = $ ▢ one and 1 tenth ▢ hundredths

19 5 tenths $= 4$ tenths ▢ hundredths

Subtract.

20
$$
\begin{array}{r}
0.36 \\
-\ 0.18 \\
\hline

\end{array}
$$

21
$$
\begin{array}{r}
2.35 \\
-\ 1.19 \\
\hline

\end{array}
$$

22
$$
\begin{array}{r}
6.20 \\
-\ 4.18 \\
\hline

\end{array}
$$

Copy and write in vertical form. Then subtract.

23 $3.85 - 1.69$ ▢

24 $16.78 - 5.9$ ▢

Learn — Add placeholder zeros to a decimal before subtracting.

Subtract 0.38 from 5.5.
You can write 5.5 as 5.50.
Write the numbers. Line up the decimal points.

Step 1
Subtract the hundredths.

$$
\begin{array}{r}
5.\overset{4}{\cancel{5}}\,{}^{1}0 \\
-\ 0.3\ 8 \\
\hline
2
\end{array}
$$

Step 2
Subtract the tenths.

$$
\begin{array}{r}
5.\overset{4}{\cancel{5}}\,{}^{1}0 \\
-\ 0.3\ 8 \\
\hline
.1\ 2
\end{array}
$$

Step 3
Subtract the ones.

$$
\begin{array}{r}
5.\overset{4}{\cancel{5}}\,{}^{1}0 \\
-\ 0.3\ 8 \\
\hline
5.1\ 2
\end{array}
$$

You cannot subtract 8 hundredths from 0 hundredths.
Regroup 5 tenths.
5 tenths $=$ 4 tenths 10 hundredths

So, $5.5 - 0.38 = 5.12$.

Guided Practice

Copy and write in vertical form. Then subtract.

25 7.5 − 3.68 [ ]

26 2 − 0.55 [ ]

Let's Practice

Subtract.

1
```
    0. 8
 −  0. 5
```
[ ]

2
```
    0. 0 9
 −  0. 0 3
```
[ ]

3
```
    5. 8 6
 −  2. 1 4
```
[ ]

Copy and write in vertical form. Then subtract.

4 7.8 − 3.4 [ ]

5 $3.94 − $2.71 [ ]

Subtract.

6
```
    1. 5
 −  0. 8
```
[ ]

7
```
    0. 4 2
 −  0. 0 7
```
[ ]

8
```
    2. 4 3
 −  1. 6 5
```
[ ]

9
```
    5. 3
 −  1. 8 6
```
[ ]

Copy and write in vertical form. Then subtract.

10 8 − 2.4 [ ]

11 24.67 − 8.79 [ ]

ON YOUR OWN

**Go to Workbook B:
Practice 3, pages 27–32**

Lesson 8.3 Real-World Problems: Decimals

Lesson Objective

- Solve real-world problems involving addition and subtraction of decimals.

Learn Solve real-world problems.

Sara has $8.50. She spends $3.75 on a book.
How much money does she have left?

$8.50 − $3.75 = $4.75

She has $4.75 left.

$$\begin{array}{r} \overset{7}{\cancel{\$8}}.\overset{^{1}4}{\cancel{5}}\,{}^{1}0 \\ -\quad \$3.7\ 5 \\ \hline \$4.7\ 5 \end{array}$$

Guided Practice

Solve. Show your work.

1 For a party, Mrs. Sun buys 2.75 liters of grape juice
and 1.26 liters of apple juice. How much fruit juice does she buy?

[   ] + [   ] = [   ]

$$\begin{array}{r} 2.7\ 5 \\ +\ 1.2\ 6 \\ \hline [\quad] \end{array}$$

She buys [   ] liters of fruit juice.

Learn Use bar models to solve real-world problems.

Peter is 0.08 meter taller than Nick. Sulin is 0.16 meter shorter than Peter.
If Sulin is 1.65 meters tall, what is Nick's height?

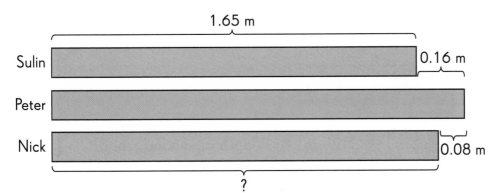

Peter's height = Sulin's height + 0.16 m
     = 1.65 + 0.16
     = 1.81 m
Peter's height is 1.81 meters.

Nick's height = Peter's height − 0.08 m
     = 1.81 − 0.08
     = 1.73 m
Nick's height is 1.73 meters.

> First, find Peter's height. Sulin is 0.16 meter shorter than Peter which means Peter is 0.16 meter taller than Sulin.

Guided Practice

Solve. Show your work.

2 A pair of pants costs $36.49. A shirt costs $24.95. Victor has $55.00.
How much more money does he need to buy the pair of pants and the shirt?
Cost of pants + cost of shirt = total cost

$ _____ + $ _____ = $ _____

The total cost of the pair of pants and the shirt is $ _____ .

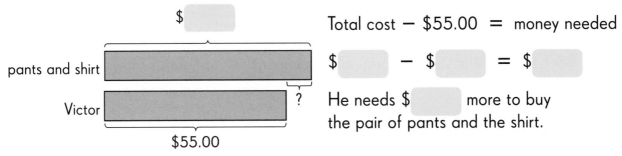

Total cost − $55.00 = money needed

$ _____ − $ _____ = $ _____

He needs $ _____ more to buy the pair of pants and the shirt.

3 A piece of fabric 4 meters long is cut into two pieces. The first piece is 1.25 meters long. How much longer is the second piece of fabric?

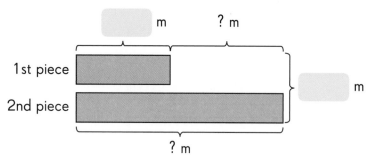

Total length of two pieces − 1.25 m = length of second piece

[ ] − [ ] = [ ]

The length of the second piece is [ ] meters.

Length of second piece − 1.25 m = difference in length between first and second pieces

[ ] − [ ] = [ ]

The second piece of fabric is [ ] meters longer.

4 Randy spent $29.85 on a soccer uniform and $18.75 on soccer equipment. He paid the cashier $50. How much change did he get?

$29.85 + $18.75 = total cost of uniform and equipment

$[ ] + $[ ] = $[ ]

The total cost of the uniform and equipment is $[ ].

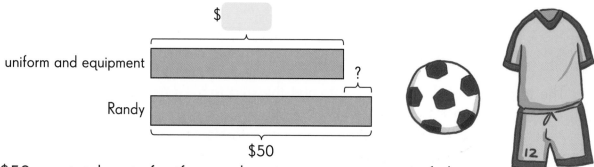

$50 − total cost of uniform and equipment = amount of change

$[ ] − $[ ] = $[ ]

He got $[ ] change.

5 Nathan jogged on Monday and Tuesday. He jogged 4.55 kilometers on Monday and 1.78 kilometers farther on Tuesday than on Monday. What was the distance he jogged on both days?

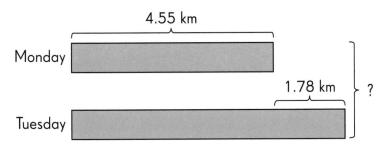

Distance jogged on Monday + 1.78 km = distance jogged on Tuesday

[   ]   +   [   ]   =   [   ]

He jogged [   ] kilometers on Tuesday.

4.55 km + distance jogged on Tuesday = distance jogged on both days

[   ]   +   [   ]   =   [   ]

He jogged [   ] kilometers on both days.

Let's Practice

1 A cup contains 72.85 milliliters of honey. A jar contains 15.2 milliliters more honey than the cup. How much honey does the jar contain?

2 Lisa spent $42.15. She spent $15.75 more than Aretha. How much did Aretha spend?

3 The weight of a watermelon is 3.6 pounds.
A pumpkin is 0.95 pound lighter than the watermelon.
What is the total weight of the pumpkin and the watermelon?

ON YOUR OWN

Go to Workbook B:
Practice 4, pages 33–34

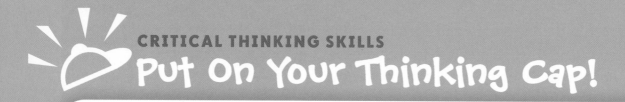
PROBLEM SOLVING

Arrange these numbers in the circles and square so that the sum of the three numbers along each line is 4.5.

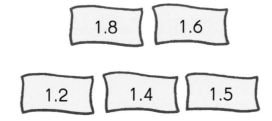

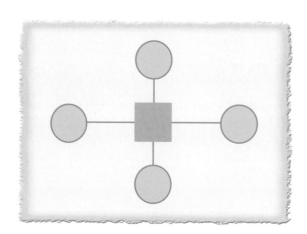

ON YOUR OWN

**Go to Workbook B:
Put on Your Thinking Cap!
pages 35–36** ▶

Chapter Wrap Up

Study Guide

You have learned...

BIG IDEA

▶ Decimals can be added and subtracted in the same ways as whole numbers.

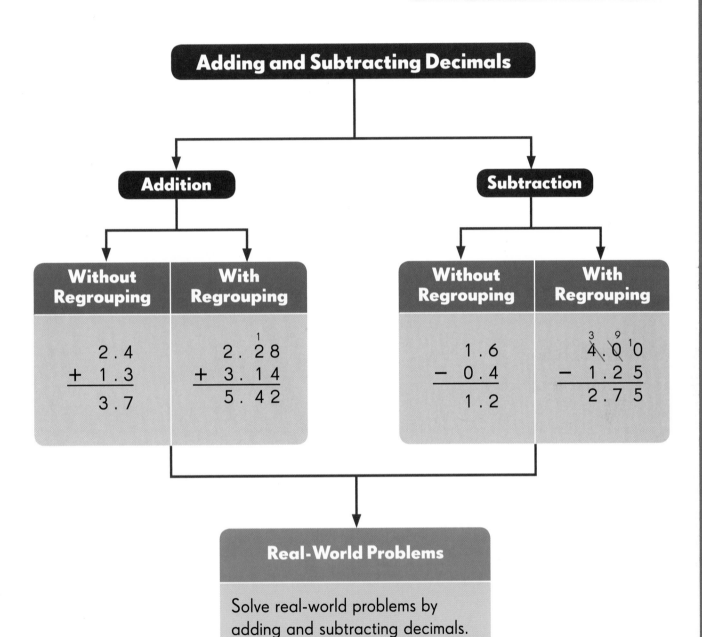

Adding and Subtracting Decimals

Addition

Subtraction

Without Regrouping

$$
\begin{array}{r}
2.4 \\
+\ 1.3 \\
\hline
3.7
\end{array}
$$

With Regrouping

$$
\begin{array}{r}
2.\overset{1}{2}8 \\
+\ 3.14 \\
\hline
5.42
\end{array}
$$

Without Regrouping

$$
\begin{array}{r}
1.6 \\
-\ 0.4 \\
\hline
1.2
\end{array}
$$

With Regrouping

$$
\begin{array}{r}
\overset{3}{4}.\overset{9}{0}\overset{1}{0} \\
-\ 1.25 \\
\hline
2.75
\end{array}
$$

Real-World Problems

Solve real-world problems by adding and subtracting decimals.

Chapter Review/Test

Concepts and Skills
Add.

1 3.47 + 6.52

2 5.04 + 3.62

3 4.8 + 2.66

4 7.93 + 4.4

5 7.05 + 1.98

6 9.81 + 8.79

Subtract.

7 8.64 − 5.01

8 6.72 − 4.32

9 6.4 − 4.23

10 11.5 − 9.45

11 9.02 − 8.77

12 30.38 − 12.62

Problem Solving
Solve. Show your work.

13 A coffee maker costs $29.90, and a toaster costs $38.90. What is their total cost?

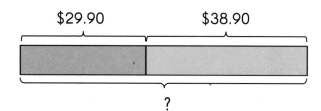

$29.90 $38.90

?

14 The perimeter of a rectangle is 28.6 centimeters less than the perimeter of a square. If the perimeter of the square is 67.2 centimeters, what is the perimeter of the rectangle?

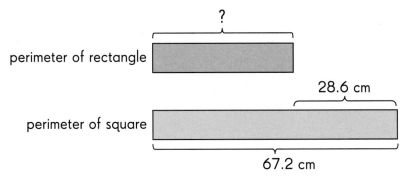

15 A length of pipe is 3.65 meters long.
Another length of pipe is 1.5 meters longer.
What is the total length of the two pipes?

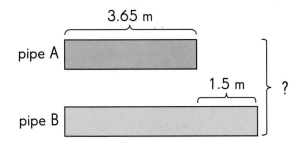

16 A tank contained 16.55 liters of water, and a jar contained 4.5 liters less. After 3.6 liters were poured out of the jar, how many liters of water were left in it?

9 Angles

Scientists have to keep track of the angle of the Leaning Tower of Pisa to make sure that it does not tip over!

Lessons

9.1 Understanding and Measuring Angles

9.2 Drawing Angles to 180°

9.3 Turns and Right Angles

BIG IDEA

▶ Angles can be seen and measured when two rays or sides of a shape meet.

Recall Prior Knowledge

Defining a point, line, and a line segment

Definition	Example	You Say and Write
A point is an exact location in space.	• A	Point B
A line is a straight path continuing without end in two opposite directions.	C ←——→ D	Line CD
A line segment is a part of a line with two endpoints.	E ———— F	Line segment EF

Defining angles

An angle is formed by two line segments with a common endpoint.

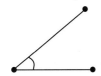

An angle can also be formed when two sides of a figure meet.

side

side

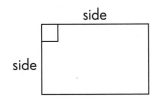

Making a right angle

Fold a piece of paper like this to get a right-angled corner.

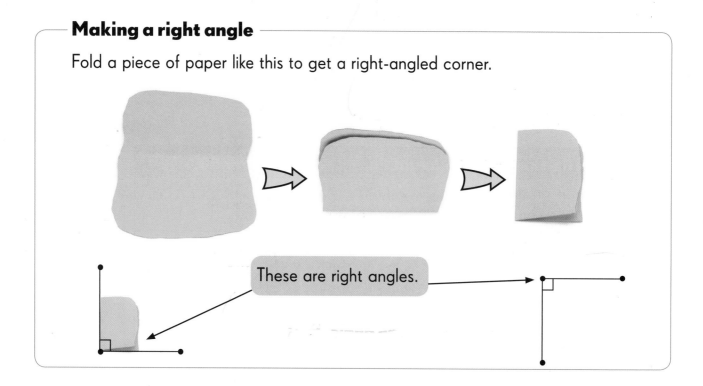

These are right angles.

Comparing angles with a right angle

Compare an angle with a right angle.

Angle *E* is the same as a right angle.

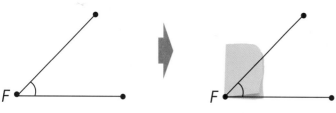

Angle *F* is less than a right angle.

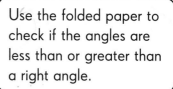

Use the folded paper to check if the angles are less than or greater than a right angle.

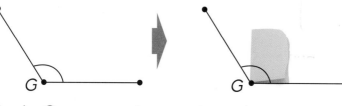

Angle *G* is greater than a right angle.

Complete with point, line, or line segment.

1 A _____ is an exact location in space.

2 A _____ is a part of a line with two endpoints.

3 A _____ is a straight path continuing without end in two opposite directions.

Decide whether each figure forms an angle. Explain your answer.

4

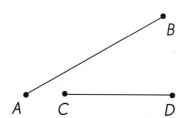

5

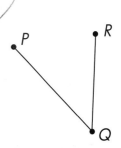

Name the angle.

6

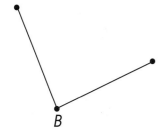

Angle _____

Copy the shapes. Mark an angle in each shape.

7 Rectangle

8 Pentagon

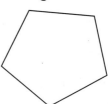

Decide whether the line segments in each angle form a right angle. Use a piece of folded paper to help you. Explain your answer.

9

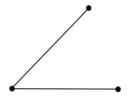

10

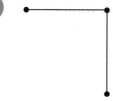

11

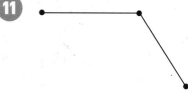

Look at the angles. Then answer the questions. Use a piece of folded paper to help you.

A

B

C

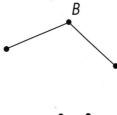

F

D

E

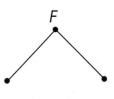

12 Which angles are right angles?

13 Which angles measure less than a right angle?

14 Which angles measure greater than a right angle?

Understanding and Measuring Angles

Lesson Objectives

- Estimate and measure angles with a protractor.
- Estimate whether the measure of an angle is less than or greater than a right angle (90°).

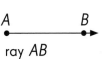 **Use letters to name rays and angles.**

A ray is part of a line that continues without end in one direction. It has one endpoint. You can use two letters to name a ray. The first letter is always the endpoint.

A ———————→ B
ray AB

You can write ray AB as $\overrightarrow{AB}$, and ray BA as $\overrightarrow{BA}$.

B ———————→ A
ray BA

In the same way, you can write:

ⓐ   line CD or DC as $\overleftrightarrow{CD}$ or $\overleftrightarrow{DC}$.

C ←———————→ D

ⓑ   line segment EF or FE as $\overline{EF}$ or $\overline{FE}$.

E ——————— F

. . . .

$\overrightarrow{PA}$ and $\overrightarrow{PB}$ are rays meeting at point P.

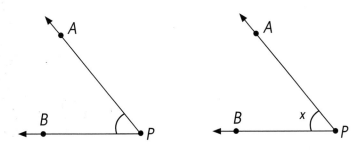

> In naming angles using three letters, the vertex is always the middle letter.

The point P is called the **vertex**.
Name the angle at vertex P ∠APB or ∠BPA.
If you label the angle at vertex P as x, you can also name it ∠x.

Guided Practice

Name the angles.

An angle is also formed by two sides of a shape meeting at a point.

1 Angle at *P*: ∠ ⬚

2 Angle at *Q*: ∠ ⬚

3 Angle at *R*: ∠ ⬚

4 Angle at *S*: ∠ ⬚

Name the angles.

5

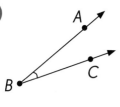

∠ ⬚

6

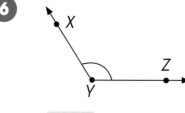

∠ ⬚

7

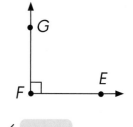

∠ ⬚

Name the angles labeled at the vertices *A*, *B*, *C*, and *D* in another way.

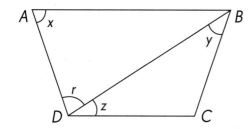

8 ∠x: ∠ ⬚

9 ∠z: ∠ ⬚

10 ∠y: ∠ ⬚

11 ∠r: ∠ ⬚

 **Hands-On Activity**

WORK IN PAIRS

Materials:
• two paper strips
• a fastener
• two sheets of
  drawing paper
• folded paper

STEP 1

Paste strip 2 on the drawing paper.
Fasten strip 1 onto strip 2 so that
only strip 1 moves. This is a pair of angle strips.

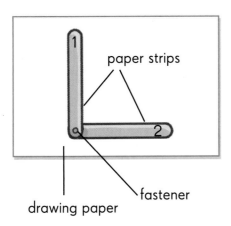

paper strips

fastener

drawing paper

STEP 2

Turn strip 1 to make these turns:

• $\frac{1}{4}$ -turn,

• $\frac{1}{2}$ -turn,

• $\frac{3}{4}$ -turn and

• a full turn.

Example

$\frac{1}{4}$ -turn: one right angle

STEP 3

Use a piece of folded paper to check
the number of right angles in each turn.

Use a protractor to measure an angle in degrees.

> An angle measure is a fraction of a full turn. An angle is measured in degrees. For example, a right angle has a measure of 90 degrees. You can write this as 90°.

You can use a protractor to measure an angle.

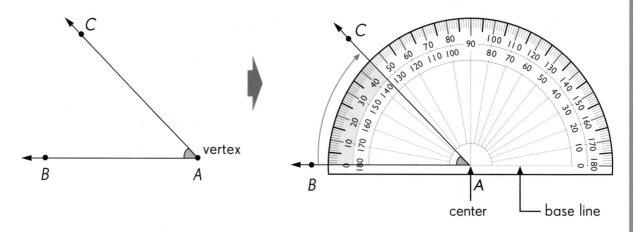

Step 1 Place the base line of the protractor on $\overrightarrow{AB}$.

Step 2 Place the center of the base line of the protractor at the vertex of the angle.

Step 3 Read the **outer scale**. $\overrightarrow{AC}$ passes through the 45° mark. So, the measure of the angle is 45°.

> Since $\overrightarrow{AB}$ passes through the zero mark of the outer scale, read the measure on the outer scale.

Measure ∠DEF.

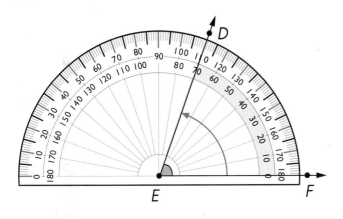

The measure of ∠DEF is less than that of a right angle.
It is 70 degrees.

Measure of ∠DEF = [ ]°

Since $\overrightarrow{EF}$ passes through the zero mark of the **inner scale**, read the measure on the inner scale.

Guided Practice

Complete.

12

B • ┐ • → C

A ↓ (with A below B)

The measure of ∠ABC is [ ] of a turn.

13

P

Q

R ← [ ]

The measure of ∠PQR is [ ] of a turn.

14 Measure ∠GHK.

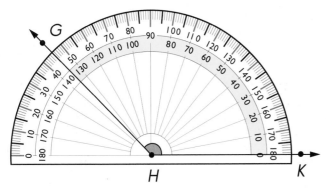

Is the measure of ∠GHK less than or greater than 90°? [ ]

The measure of ∠GHK is [ ] degrees.

Measure of ∠GHK = [ ]°

Explain when to use the inner scale of the protractor.

15 Measure ∠JKL.

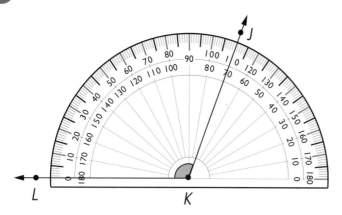

Is the measure of ∠JKL less than or greater than 90°? ▢

The measure of ∠JKL is ▢ degrees.

Measure of ∠JKL = ▢ °

Did you read the inner or outer scale? Explain your answer.

Find the measure of each angle.

16

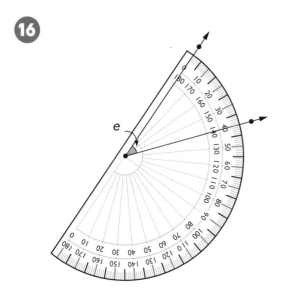

Measure of ∠e = ▢ °

17

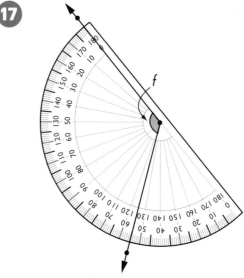

Measure of ∠f = ▢ °

An angle with a measure less than 90° is an **acute angle**.

An angle with a measure greater than 90° but less than 180° is an **obtuse angle**.

So, ∠e is an ▢ angle, and ∠f is an ▢ angle.

 **Hands-On Activity**

Material:
• protractor

WORK IN PAIRS

Estimate the measure of each angle by comparing it to a right angle (90°). Then measure each one with a protractor.
Decide if each angle is an acute angle, an obtuse angle, or a right angle.

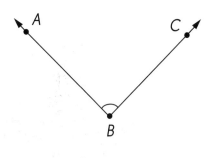

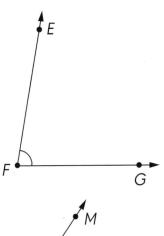

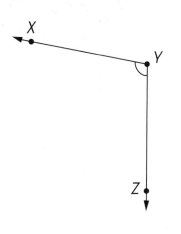

Record your answers in a table like this.

Angle	Estimated Measure	Actual Measure	Type of Angle
∠ABC	80°	90°	Right Angle

READING AND WRITING MATH
Math Journal

The steps for measuring these angles are not in order.
Arrange the steps in order by using 1, 2, or 3 in each box.

1 Obtuse angle

C

A   *x*

B

Step [ ] Place the center of the base line of the protractor at vertex *B* of the angle.

Step [ ] Place the base line of the protractor on ray *BA*.

Step [ ] Read the outer scale at the point where ray *BC* crosses it.
The reading is 116°.
So, the angle measure is 116°.

2 Acute angle

M

y

N   *O*

Step [ ] Read the inner scale at the point where ray *NM* crosses it.
The reading is 50°.
So, the angle measure is 50°.

Step [ ] Place the base line of the protractor on ray *NO*.

Step [ ] Place the center of the base line of the protractor at vertex *N* of the angle.

3 **Compare the measures of the two angles in Exercises 1 and 2.**
Use < and > in your answers.

Let's Practice

Name and measure the angles.

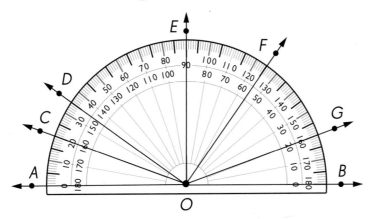

1 Name two angles that are right angles.

2 Name four angles that are acute angles. What are the measures of these angles?

3 Name four angles that are obtuse angles. What are the measures of these angles?

Use a protractor to find the measure of each angle.

4

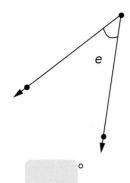

e

5

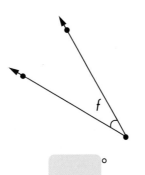

f

6

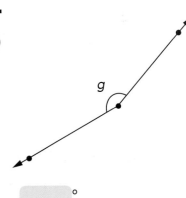

g

Use a protractor to measure each marked angle.

7

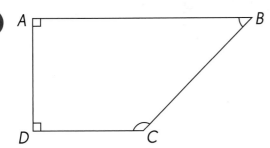

ON YOUR OWN

Go to Workbook B:
Practice 1, pages 45–50

Lesson 9.2 Drawing Angles to 180°

Lesson Objective

- Use a protractor to draw acute and obtuse angles.

Vocabulary
acute angle
obtuse angle
straight angle

Learn **Use a protractor to draw acute and obtuse angles.**

Follow these steps to draw an angle of 70°.

Step 1 Draw a line and mark a point on the line. This point is the vertex.

vertex

Step 2 Place the base line of the protractor on the line and the center of the base line on the vertex.

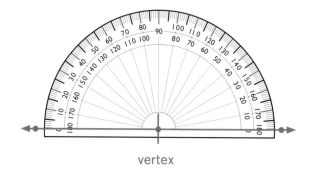

vertex

Step 3 Use the inner scale or the outer scale to find the 70° mark. Mark it with a dot as shown. Then draw a ray from the vertex through the dot.

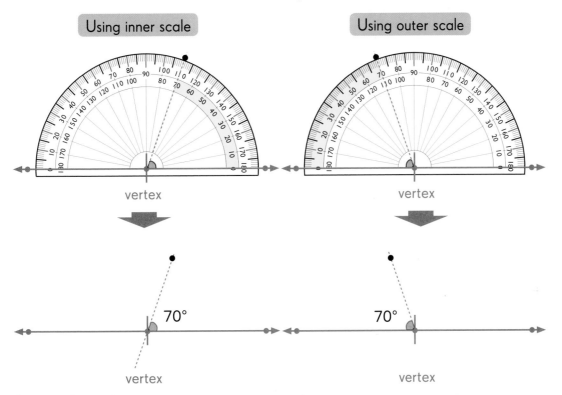

This is how you draw an angle measure of 145°.
Remember to start by lining up the vertex and the base line.

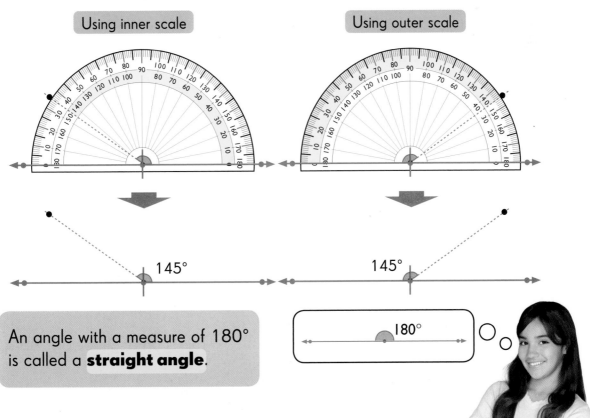

An angle with a measure of 180° is called a **straight angle**.

180°

Hands-On Activity

Material:
• protractor

Use a protractor to draw angles with these measures:

1 greater than 90° but less than 125°.

2 greater than 10° but less than 25°.

3 greater than 100° but less than 180°.

Example

An angle measure greater than 30° but less than 60°.

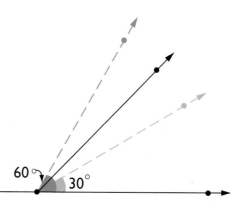

Learn **Angles can be drawn in different directions.**

Draw a ray and label it $\overrightarrow{AB}$.
Using point A as the vertex, draw $\angle CAB$ that measures:

a 45° so that $\overrightarrow{AC}$ lies above $\overrightarrow{AB}$.

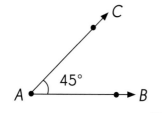

This is an angle above $\overrightarrow{AB}$.

b 45° so that $\overrightarrow{AC}$ lies below $\overrightarrow{AB}$.

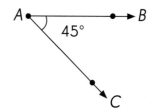

This is an angle below $\overrightarrow{AB}$.

Guided Practice

Use a protractor to draw angles.

Draw a ray and label it $\overrightarrow{QP}$. Using point Q as the vertex, draw $\angle PQR$ that measures:

1 55° so that $\overrightarrow{QP}$ lies above $\overrightarrow{QR}$.

2 55° so that $\overrightarrow{QP}$ lies below $\overrightarrow{QR}$.

Let's Practice

On a copy of these line segments, use a protractor to draw angles.

1 On $\overleftrightarrow{AB}$, draw an angle measure greater than 45° but less than 90° at point C.

2 On $\overleftrightarrow{CD}$, draw an angle measure of 125° at point E.

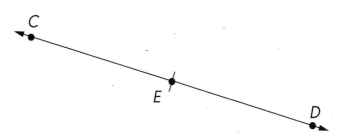

Complete.

3 The measure of $\angle DEF$ is 140°. Draw and label the angle.

4 Draw:
  a a right angle.
  b an acute angle.
  c an obtuse angle.

ON YOUR OWN

Go to Workbook B: Practice 2, pages 51–54

9.3 Turns and Right Angles

Lesson Objective

- Relate $\frac{1}{4}$ -, $\frac{1}{2}$ -, $\frac{3}{4}$ - and full turns to the number of right angles (90°).

Vocabulary
turn
straight angle

Learn **Relate turns to right angles.**

One right angle

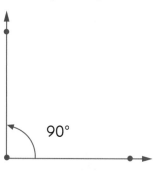

90°

A $\frac{1}{4}$ -turn is 90°.

Two right angles

An angle that is 180° is also known as a **straight angle**.

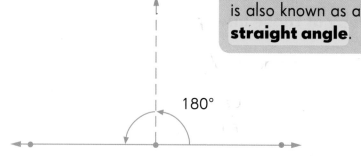

180°

A $\frac{1}{2}$ -turn is 180°.

Three right angles

270°

A $\frac{3}{4}$ -turn is 270°.

Four right angles

360°

A full turn is 360°.

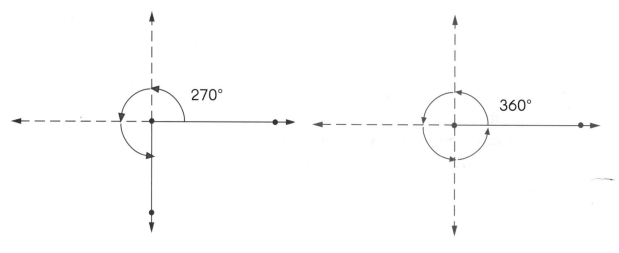

Hands-On Activity

Refer to the Hands-On Activity on page 87.

STEP 1 Use a pair of angle strips to make $\frac{1}{4}$ -, $\frac{1}{2}$ -, $\frac{3}{4}$ -, and full turns again.

STEP 2 On a separate sheet of paper, draw and label the angle formed in each turn in **STEP 1**. Relate each angle to

a a fraction of a full turn.

b the number of right angles. Then give its measure.

An angle measure is a fraction of a full turn. The value is given in degrees.

Example

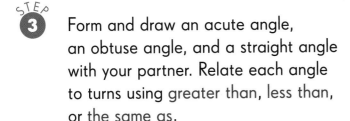

Measure of $\angle d$: $\frac{1}{4}$ -turn

one right angle
90°

d

STEP 3 Form and draw an acute angle, an obtuse angle, and a straight angle with your partner. Relate each angle to turns using greater than, less than, or the same as.

Guided Practice

Complete.

1 Two right angles make up a [   ] -turn.

2 Four right angles is the same as [   ] full turn.

3 270° is [   ] of a full turn.

4 93° is between a [   ] -turn and a [   ] -turn.

5 200° is between a [   ] -turn and a [   ] -turn.

Let's Practice

Use the pair of angle strips you made to answer the questions.

1 How many turns are in three right angles? [   ]

2 How many turns are in four right angles? [   ]

3 What fraction of a full turn is two right angles? [   ]

Use the pair of angle strips to form these angles.
Draw each angle on a piece of paper.

4 Angle between a $\frac{3}{4}$ -turn and a full turn.

5 Angle between a $\frac{1}{2}$ -turn and a full turn.

6 Angle between a $\frac{1}{4}$ -turn and a $\frac{1}{2}$ -turn.

ON YOUR OWN

Go to Workbook B:
Practice 3, pages 55–58

Put On Your Thinking Cap!

PROBLEM SOLVING

Joshua stands in the center of the circle shown in the picture.

1. If Joshua is facing Blake and he turns around until he is looking at Ian, what fraction of a turn will he make?

2. What angle does Joshua turn through if he moves:

   a. from looking at Perry to looking at Ian?

   b. from looking at Roy to looking at Perry?

3. What angle does Joshua turn through if he completes a $\frac{3}{4}$ -turn?

ON YOUR OWN

**Go to Workbook B:
Put on Your Thinking Cap!
pages 59–60**

Chapter Wrap Up

Study Guide
You have learned...

[Angles]

Name Angles

Name the angle at vertex B as $\angle ABC$, $\angle CBA$, or $\angle x$.

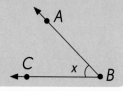

Measure Acute and Obtuse Angles

An angle measure is a fraction of a full turn. An angle is measured in degrees.
The measure of $\angle ABC$ is 45°.

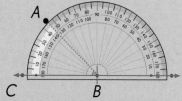

The measure of $\angle DEF$ is 145°.

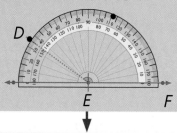

Draw Angles

Use inner scale   Use outer scale

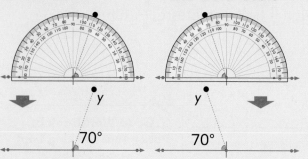

Relate Turns and Right Angles

$\frac{1}{4}$ -turn is one right angle or 90°.

$\frac{1}{2}$ -turn is two right angles or 180°.

A straight angle is 180°.

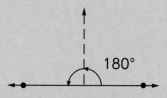

$\frac{3}{4}$ -turn is three right angles or 270°.

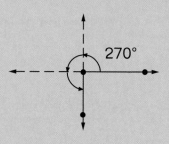

One full turn is four right angles or 360°.

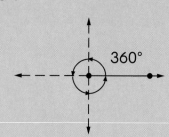

Chapter Review/Test

Vocabulary

Choose the correct word.

1 When two ▢ meet, they form an angle.

2 The ▢ is the point where two rays meet.

3 Use a ▢ to measure an angle.

acute angle	protractor
obtuse angle	degrees
straight angle	turn
rays	inner scale
vertex	outer scale

Concepts and Skills

Find the correct ray.

4 Which ray forms an angle measure of 85° with ray *AX*? ▢

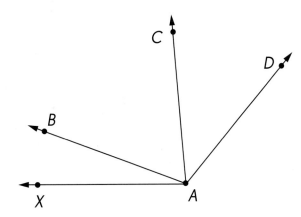

5 Which ray forms an angle measure of 120° with ray *PQ*? ▢

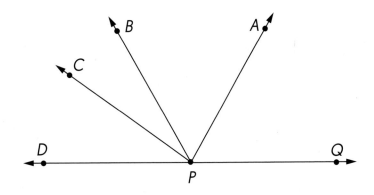

Draw.

6 Draw a triangle. Name the vertices of the triangle *A*, *B*, and *C*.
Write *x*, *y*, and *z* inside the triangle so that:

∠*x* is ∠*BAC*,
∠*y* is ∠*ACB*, and
∠*z* is ∠*ABC*.

Which scale would you use to read the angles shown?
Use inner scale or outer scale.

7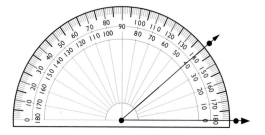

8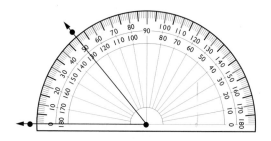

Use a protractor to measure the angles.
Then identify the acute angles and obtuse angles.

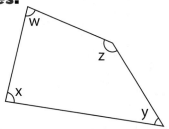

9 Measure of ∠*w* = ⬚°

10 Measure of ∠*x* = ⬚°

11 Measure of ∠*y* = ⬚°

12 Measure of ∠*z* = ⬚°

Draw angles with these measures.

13 64°

14 170°

Fill in the blanks.

15 $\frac{3}{4}$ -turn is ⬚°.

16 90° is ⬚ -turn.

17 One full turn is ⬚°.

10

Perpendicular and Parallel Line Segments

Lessons

BIG IDEA

▶ Line segments can go up and down, from side to side, and in every direction.

Recall Prior Knowledge

Checking perpendicular lines

Perpendicular lines are two lines that meet at a right angle or 90°.

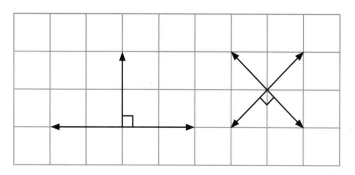

Use a folded sheet of paper or a ruler to check whether two lines are perpendicular.

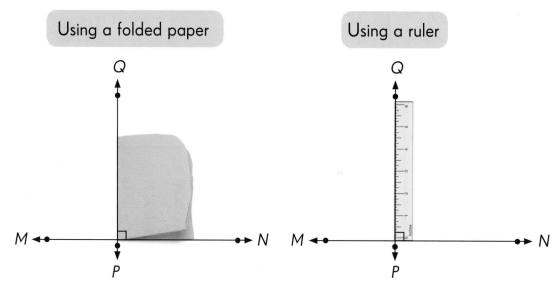

Using a folded paper

Using a ruler

Line *PQ* is perpendicular to line *MN*.

Checking parallel lines

Parallel lines are a set of lines that will never meet no matter how long they are drawn. They are always the same distance apart.

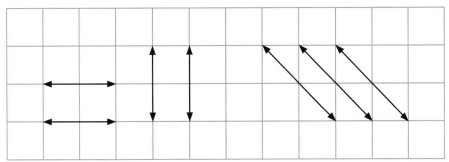

Finding perpendicular lines in everyday objects

These are perpendicular line segments in everyday objects.

Finding parallel lines in everyday objects

These are parallel lines in everyday objects.

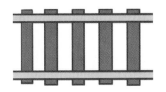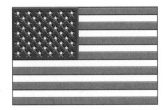

Copying perpendicular lines on grid paper

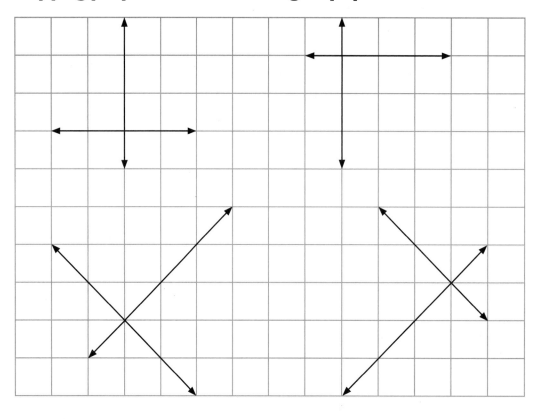

Copying parallel lines on grid paper

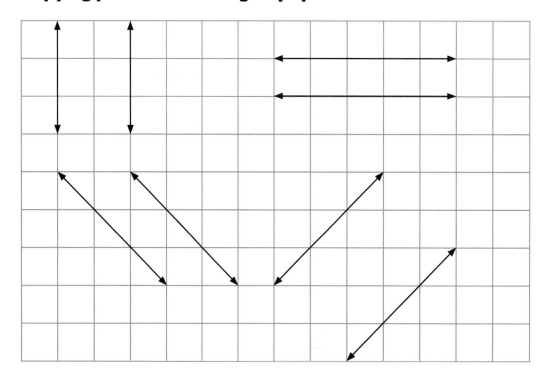

Which pairs of line segments are perpendicular?
Use a folded sheet of paper or straightedge to check.

1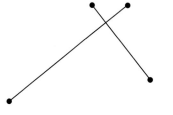

2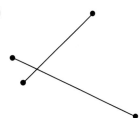

3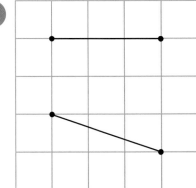

4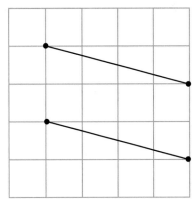

Which pairs of line segments are parallel?

5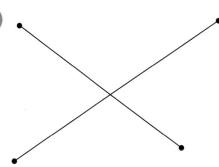

6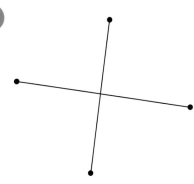

7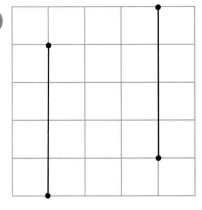

8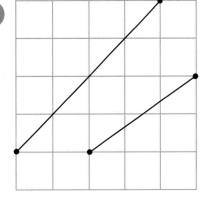

Complete with **perpendicular or parallel.**

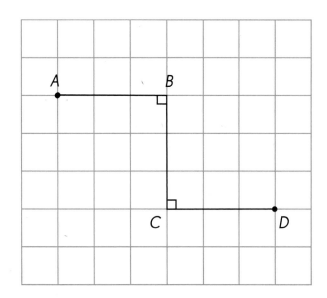

9   $\overline{AB}$ is ▢ to $\overline{CD}$.

10 $\overline{AB}$ is ▢ to $\overline{BC}$.

11 $\overline{BC}$ is ▢ to $\overline{CD}$.

Name a pair of perpendicular line segments and a pair of parallel line segments.

12
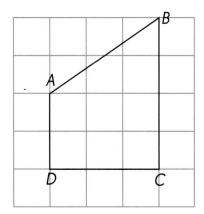

13
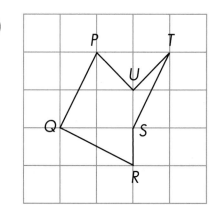

Identify the perpendicular line segments and the parallel line segments on this picture frame.

14
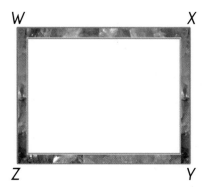

Drawing Perpendicular Line Segments

Lesson Objective

- Draw perpendicular line segments.

Vocabulary
perpendicular line segments (⊥)
drawing triangle

Learn **Use a protractor to draw a line segment perpendicular to segment *AB*.**

Step 1 Mark a point on $\overline{AB}$ and label it *C*.
Place the base line of the protractor on $\overline{AB}$.
Align the center of the base line with point *C*.
Use the inner or outer scale to find the 90° mark.

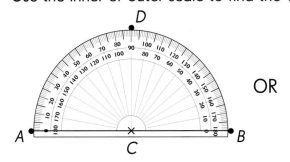

OR

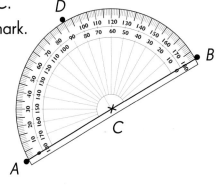

Step 2 Use a straightedge to connect point *C* and point *D*.

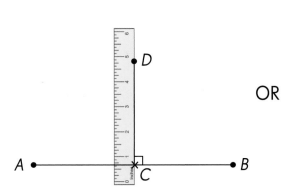

OR

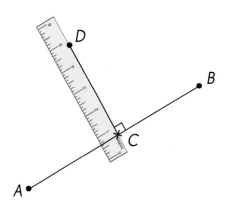

$\overline{AB}$ and $\overline{CD}$ are **perpendicular line segments**.
You can write this as $\overline{AB} \perp \overline{CD}$.

Learn **Use a drawing triangle to draw a line segment perpendicular to segment _AB_.**

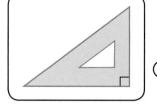

Step 1 Mark a point _C_ on $\overline{AB}$.

Place the straightedge of the drawing triangle on $\overline{AB}$ to align its right-angled corner with point _C_.

Mark a point vertically above point _C_ along the straightedge of the drawing triangle. Label this point _D_.

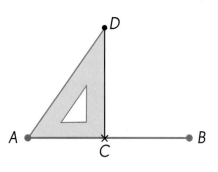

OR

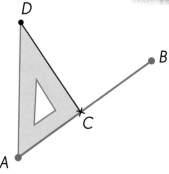

Step 2 Connect point _C_ and point _D_.

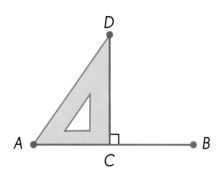

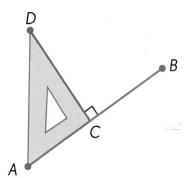

$\overline{AB}$ and $\overline{CD}$ are perpendicular line segments.

$\overline{AB} \perp \overline{CD}$

 **Hands-On Activity**

Materials:
• straightedge
• grid paper

WORK IN PAIRS

1. Use a straightedge to draw a line segment. Ask your partner to draw a line segment perpendicular to yours. Reverse roles and repeat.

2. Use grid paper as shown. Draw a line segment perpendicular to $\overline{AB}$ and $\overline{CD}$ without using a protractor. Explain how you drew the line segments.

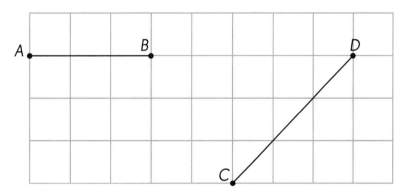

Guided Practice

Copy the line segments. Draw a line segment perpendicular to the given line segment through points *A* and *B*.

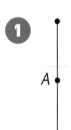

1.

A

2.

B

Copy the line segments. Draw a line segment perpendicular to the given line segment.

3.

4.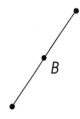

Let's Practice

Look at the figure.

1 Copy the figure. Draw a line segment perpendicular to $\overline{AB}$ and passing through point B.

2 Draw a line segment perpendicular to $\overline{AD}$ and passing through point D.

3 Extend each line segment you drew in Exercises 1 and 2 until they meet. Label this point C.

What do you notice about the two line segments you have drawn?
What shape did you form?

Complete the figure.

4 Figure A is made up of two identical squares. Copy and complete the figure on the right to form a figure identical to figure A.

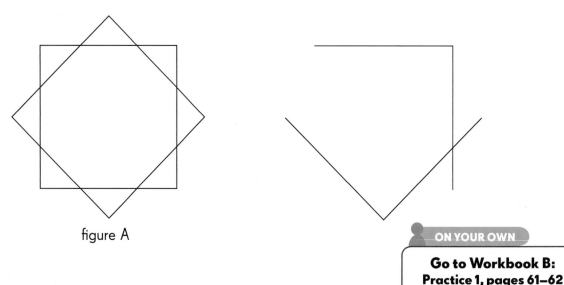

figure A

ON YOUR OWN

Go to Workbook B:
Practice 1, pages 61–62

Lesson 10.2 Drawing Parallel Line Segments

Lesson Objective
- Draw parallel line segments.

Vocabulary
parallel line segments (||)
base

Learn **Draw a line segment parallel to segment *PQ*.**

Step 1 Place a drawing triangle against $\overline{PQ}$.

Then place a straightedge at the **base** of the drawing triangle.

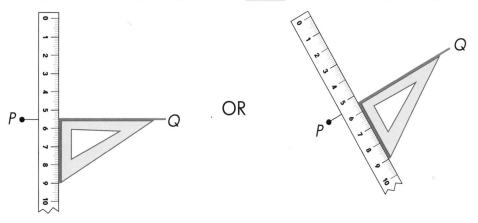

OR

Step 2 Slide the drawing triangle along the straightedge.

Then use the edge of the drawing triangle to draw $\overline{MN}$.

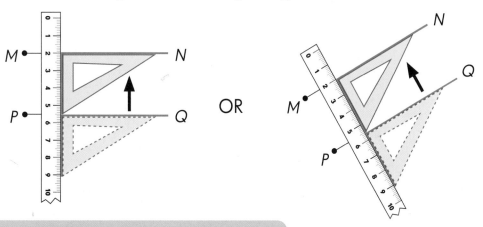

OR

$\overline{PQ}$ and $\overline{MN}$ are **parallel line segments**.

You can write this as $\overline{PQ}$ || $\overline{MN}$.

Draw a parallel line segment that goes through a given point.

Draw a line segment parallel to $\overline{CD}$ through point R.

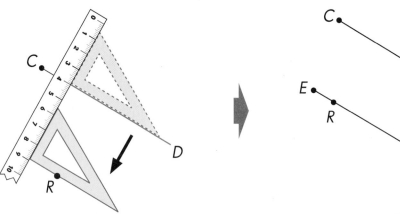

$\overline{EF}$ is parallel to $\overline{CD}$.

$\overline{EF} \parallel \overline{CD}$

Slide the drawing triangle along the straightedge until the edge of the drawing triangle touches point R. Then draw a line through point R.

Guided Practice

Copy triangle *PQR* on a sheet of paper. Then follow the directions.

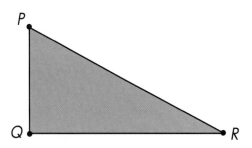

Use a drawing triangle and a straightedge to draw

1 a line segment parallel to $\overline{QR}$ through point P.

2 a line segment parallel to $\overline{PQ}$ through point R.

3 Extend each line segment you drew in Exercises 1 and 2 until they meet. What do you notice about the two line segments you have drawn?

4 What do you notice about the figure you have drawn?

 Hands-On Activity

WORK IN PAIRS

Materials:
- straightedge
- drawing triangle

1 Use a straightedge to draw a line segment.
Ask your partner to draw a line segment parallel to yours.
Reverse roles and repeat.

2 Use a straightedge to draw a line segment.
Then mark a point near it.
Ask your partner to draw a line segment parallel to
the first line segment through the point. Reverse roles and repeat.

3 On a sheet of paper, copy $\overline{EF}$ and the dots as shown.
Draw line segments parallel to $\overline{EF}$. Each line segment
you draw should pass through one of the given points.

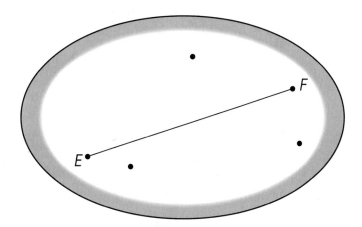

Let's Practice

Complete.

1 Use a drawing triangle and a straightedge to draw a line segment parallel to $\overline{TU}$ through point V.

2 Use a drawing triangle and a straightedge to draw a line segment parallel to $\overline{AB}$ through point C.

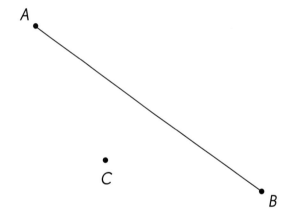

Complete the pattern.

3 Copy the figure. Draw parallel line segments to complete the figure. Color the correct rungs to complete the figure.

ON YOUR OWN

**Go to Workbook B:
Practice 2, pages 63–64**

Lesson 10.3 Horizontal and Vertical Lines

Lesson Objective

- Identify horizontal and vertical lines.

Vocabulary
horizontal lines
vertical lines

Learn Identify horizontal and vertical lines.

Two pairs of parallel lines are drawn on a sheet of paper and pinned on a wall.

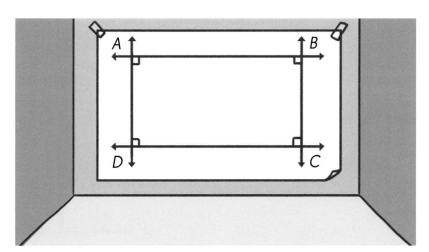

A vertical line is always perpendicular to a horizontal line.

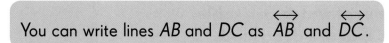

You can write lines AB and DC as $\overleftrightarrow{AB}$ and $\overleftrightarrow{DC}$.

$\overleftrightarrow{AB}$ and $\overleftrightarrow{DC}$ are parallel to the floor.

Both $\overleftrightarrow{AB}$ and $\overleftrightarrow{DC}$ are **horizontal lines**.

$\overleftrightarrow{AD}$ and $\overleftrightarrow{BC}$ meet the horizontal lines AB and DC at right angles.

Both $\overleftrightarrow{AD}$ and $\overleftrightarrow{BC}$ are **vertical lines**.

Guided Practice

Look at the picture below. Find the vertical and horizontal line segments. Describe these line segments using the terms vertical, horizontal, parallel, and perpendicular.

Complete with horizontal or vertical.

2 Angela placed a stick *XY* upright on the ground.

The stick *XY* is a [ ] line segment.

The line *AB* on the ground is a [ ] line.

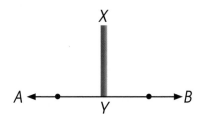

The picture shows a container of water on a table. Name all the line segments that are described.

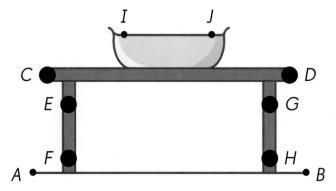

3 Horizontal line segments: [ ]

4 Vertical line segments: [ ]

Let's Practice

Look at each picture.

1 Identify the vertical line segments.

2 Identify the horizontal line segments.

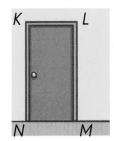

ON YOUR OWN

Go to Workbook B:
Practice 3, pages 65–68

CRITICAL THINKING SKILLS
Put on Your Thinking Cap!

PROBLEM SOLVING

X is a point not on $\overline{AB}$.

• X

A •————————————————• B

Use a protractor, a drawing triangle, and a straightedge.

STEP 1 Copy $\overline{AB}$ and point X on a piece of paper.

STEP 2 Draw a line segment perpendicular to $\overline{AB}$ through point X.

STEP 3 Draw two more line segments to make a rectangle.

ON YOUR OWN

Go to Workbook B:
Put on Your Thinking Cap!
pages 69–72

Chapter Wrap Up

Study Guide

You have learned...

Lines and Line Segments

Perpendicular and Parallel Line Segments

Draw a line segment perpendicular to a given line segment
- through a point on the given line segment (use a drawing triangle and protractor).
- through a point not on the given line segment (use a drawing triangle).

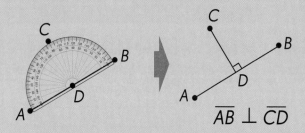

$\overline{AB} \perp \overline{CD}$

Draw a line segment parallel to
- a given line segment.
- a given line segment and passing through a given point.

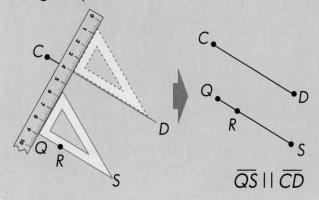

$\overline{QS} \parallel \overline{CD}$

Horizontal and Vertical Lines

Understand the terms horizontal and vertical lines.
Know that
- all lines parallel to level ground are horizontal.
- all lines perpendicular to level ground are vertical.

Identify horizontal and vertical lines in given figures and in your surroundings.

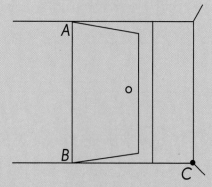

$\overline{BC}$ is a horizontal line segment.

$\overline{AB}$ is a vertical line segment.

Chapter Review/Test

Vocabulary

Choose the correct word.

perpendicular
parallel
base
drawing triangle
vertical
horizontal

1 When two line segments meet at right angles, they are _____ to each other.

2 Two _____ line segments are parts of lines that are the same distance apart.

3 A line segment perpendicular to level ground is a _____ line segment.

4 A line segment parallel to level ground is a _____ line segment.

Concepts and Skills

Complete with yes or no.

5 $\overline{PQ}$ is perpendicular to $\overline{RS}$.

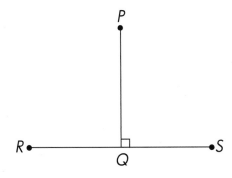

If $\overline{PQ}$ is vertical, must $\overline{RS}$ be horizontal? _____

6 $\overline{AB}$ is perpendicular to $\overline{BC}$.

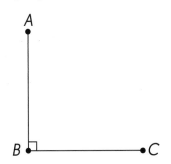

If $\overline{BC}$ is horizontal, must $\overline{AB}$ be vertical? _____

Copy the line segments.

7 Draw a line segment perpendicular to $\overline{XY}$ through point Y.

8 Draw a line segment perpendicular to $\overline{PQ}$ through point O.

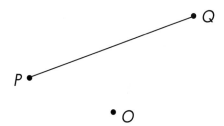

9 Draw a line segment parallel to $\overline{AB}$.

10 Draw a line segment parallel to $\overline{QR}$ through point P.

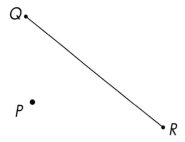

11 Squares and Rectangles

What objects are square or rectangular in shape?

Lessons

11.1 Squares and Rectangles

11.2 Properties of Squares and Rectangles

BIG IDEA

▶ Squares and rectangles are four-sided figures with special properties.

Identifying squares and rectangles

square and
rectangle

rectangle

rectangle

square and
rectangle

Rectangles
- Opposite sides are parallel, and are of the same length.
- All angles measure 90°.
- A rectangle may or may not be a square.

Squares
- All sides are of the same length.
- Opposite sides are parallel.
- All angles measure 90°.
- A square is a special type of rectangle.

Breaking up shapes made up of squares and rectangles

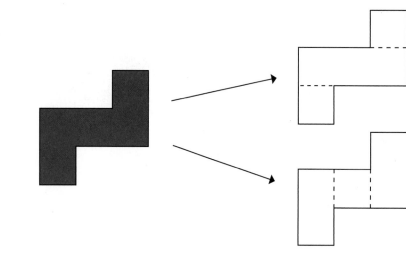

Finding the perimeter of a square and a rectangle

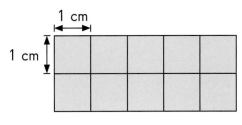

The perimeter of a figure is the distance around it.
So, the perimeter of the square is 12 centimeters.
The perimeter of the rectangle is 14 centimeters.

 Quick Check

Identify the squares and rectangles.

1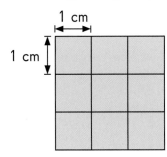
2
3
4

Break up each shape into squares and rectangles in two ways.

5
6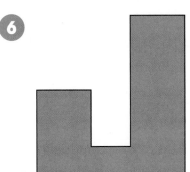
7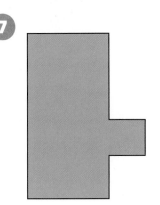

Complete.

8 Figure *ABCD* is a square.

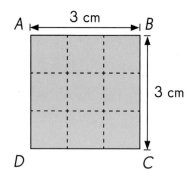

It has four sides of the same length. ◻ = ◻ = ◻ = ◻

Its opposite sides are parallel. ◻ || ◻ and ◻ || ◻

It has four right angles. Each angle measures ◻°.

The perimeter of figure *ABCD* is ◻ centimeters.

9 Figure *EFGH* is a rectangle.

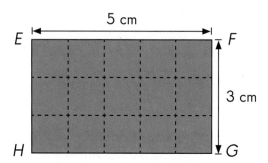

It has four sides.
Its opposite sides are parallel, and are of the same length.

◻ = ◻ and ◻ = ◻

◻ || ◻ and ◻ || ◻

It has ◻ right angles. Each angle measures 90°.

The perimeter of figure *EFGH* is ◻ centimeters.

11.1 Squares and Rectangles

Lesson Objective

- Understand and apply the properties of squares and rectangles.

Learn **Identify a square and its properties.**

This is a square.

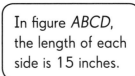

A square is a four-sided figure.
It has four sides of the same length.

$AB = BC = CD = DA$

 The tick marks show that the lengths of all sides are equal.

In figure *ABCD*, the length of each side is 15 inches.

Its opposite sides are **parallel**.
So, a square has two pairs of parallel sides.

$\overline{AB} \parallel \overline{DC}$ and $\overline{AD} \parallel \overline{BC}$

It has four **right angles**.
Measure of $\angle a$ = measure of $\angle b$
= measure of $\angle c$ = measure of $\angle d$
= 90°

^Learn   Identify a rectangle and its properties.

This is a rectangle.

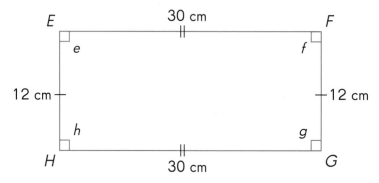

A rectangle is a four-sided figure.

Its opposite sides are of equal length.
EF = *HG* and *EH* = *FG*

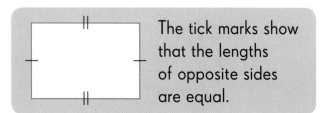
The tick marks show
that the lengths
of opposite sides
are equal.

In figure *EFGH*,
the length of $\overline{EF}$ and
$\overline{GH}$ is 30 centimeters.
The length of $\overline{EH}$ and
$\overline{FG}$ is 12 centimeters.

Its opposite sides are parallel.
So, a rectangle has two pairs of parallel sides.
$\overline{EF} \parallel \overline{HG}$ and $\overline{EH} \parallel \overline{FG}$

It has four right angles.
Measure of ∠*e* = measure of ∠*f*
= measure of ∠*g* = measure of ∠*h*
= 90°

Guided Practice

Look at the figures on the grid.

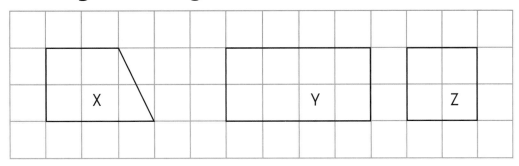

Check (✓) the boxes to show the properties of each figure on the grid.

Property	Figure		
	X	**Y**	**Z**
1 Has four sides	✓	✓	✓
2 All sides are of equal length			
3 Opposite sides are of equal length			
4 Has exactly one pair of parallel sides			
5 Has exactly two pairs of parallel sides			
6 Has exactly four right angles			
7 Has exactly two right angles			

Use the properties in Exercises 1 to 7 to identify the figures on the grid.

8 Figure _____ is a rectangle and a square.

9 Figure _____ is a rectangle but not a square.

10 Figure _____ is not a square or a rectangle.

Tell which figure is a square. Explain how to identify a square.

 11

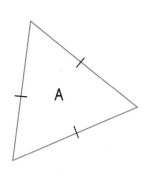

A

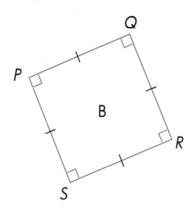

P   Q

B

R

S

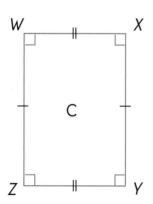

C

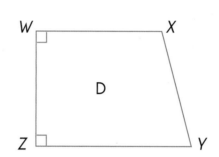

W   X

D

Z   Y

Tell which figure is a rectangle. Explain how to identify a rectangle.

 12

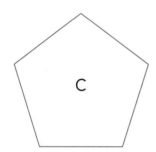

P   Q

A

S   R

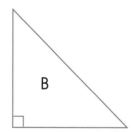

B

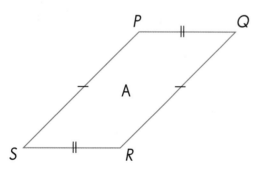

W   X

C

Z   Y

D

Hands-On Activity

Use a geoboard and a rubber band
to form these figures.
You may copy the shapes onto
square dot paper.
Then use a drawing triangle and a protractor
to help you identify the shapes.
Which figures are squares?
Which figures are rectangles?

1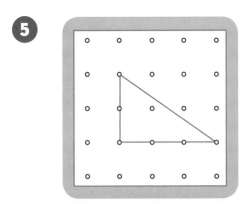

2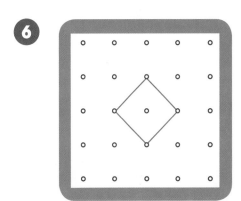

3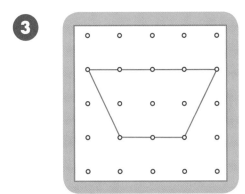

4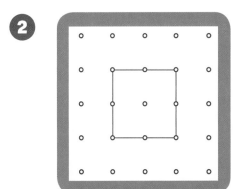

5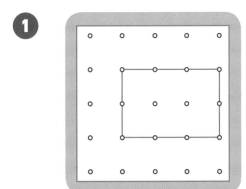

6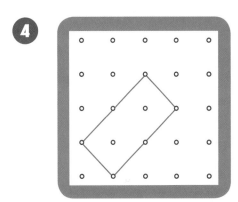

Guided Practice

Find the lengths of the unknown sides.

13 Figure *JKLM* is a square.

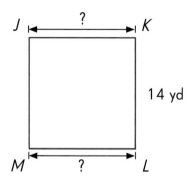

JK = ▢ yd

LM = ▢ yd

14 Figure *PQRS* is a rectangle.

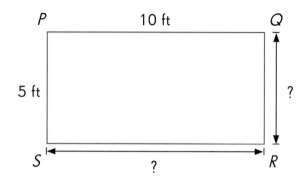

QR = ▢ ft

RS = ▢ ft

Learn **Some figures can be broken up into squares and rectangles.**

This figure can be broken up into one square and one rectangle.

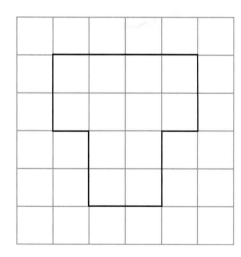

Can you break up the figure in another way?

Guided Practice

Copy these figures on grid paper.
Draw line segments to break up each figure into square(s) and rectangle(s).

15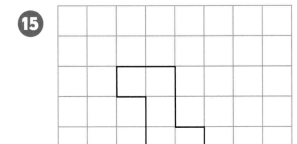

16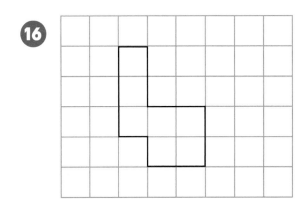

 Hands-On Activity

Materials:
- geoboard
- four rubber bands

1 Use a geoboard and two rubber bands. Form a figure that is made up of a square and a rectangle with no overlap.

Example

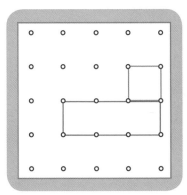

2 Form each figure on the geoboard. Each figure should have more than four sides.

a a figure made up of two rectangles

b a figure made up of one rectangle and two squares

c a figure made up of one square and two rectangles

d a figure made up of four squares

e a figure made up of four rectangles

Hands-On Activity

Materials:
• strips of centimeter grid paper

3 Use strips of paper with these lengths:
4 cm, 4 cm, 4 cm, 4 cm, 6 cm, 6 cm, 6 cm, 6 cm, 8 cm, 8 cm.

STEP
1 Use your strips to form two squares and two rectangles.
Use only one or two strips to form each side of the shapes.

STEP
2 Draw the shapes on a piece of paper.
Label the lengths of the sides.

STEP
3 Compare your shapes with the shapes formed
by the other groups.
How many different sizes of squares and rectangles
can you find?

4 Use a computer drawing tool to draw these figures.
Each figure is formed by a square and a rectangle.

Tech Connection

a

b

c

d

Let's Practice

Identify the squares and rectangles.

1

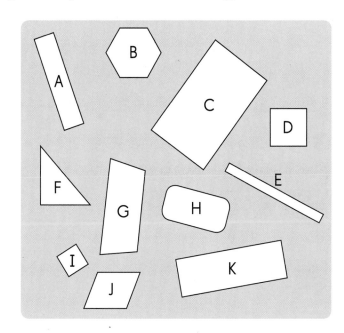

Find the lengths of the unknown sides of the squares and rectangles.

2

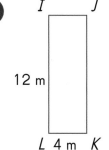

AD = [   ] cm

BC = [   ] cm

DC = [   ] cm

3

EF = [   ] in.

EH = [   ] in.

HG = [   ] in.

4

IJ = [   ] m

JK = [   ] m

5

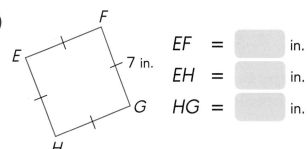

NO = [   ] mi

PO = [   ] mi

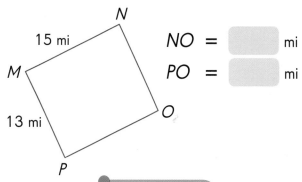

ON YOUR OWN

Go to Workbook B:
Practice 1, pages 73–76

Copy these figures on grid paper. Draw a line segment to break up each figure into a square and a rectangle.

 6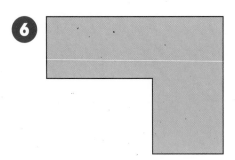

7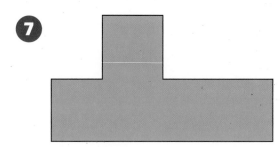

Copy these figures on grid paper. Draw line segments to break up each figure into two squares and one rectangle.

8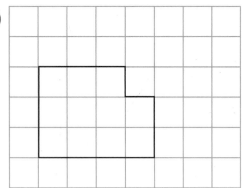

9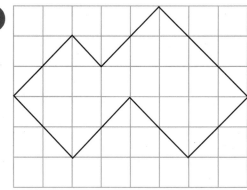

Copy these figures on grid paper. Draw line segments to break up each figure into one square and two rectangles.

10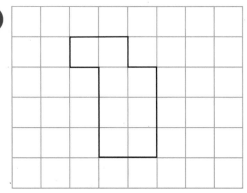

11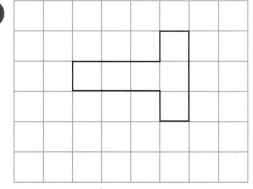

Properties of Squares and Rectangles

Lesson Objective

• Find unknown angle measures and side lengths of squares and rectangles.

Learn **Use the properties of squares and rectangles to find angle measures.**

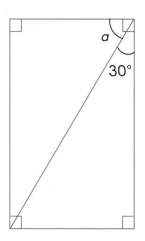

A square or a rectangle has four right angles.

Find the measure of $\angle a$.

Measure of $\angle a$ = $90° - 30°$
= $60°$

Guided Practice

Find the unknown measures of the angles in the square and rectangle.

1

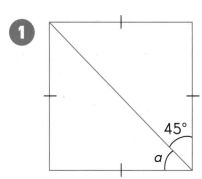

Measure of $\angle a$ = ⬚ °

2

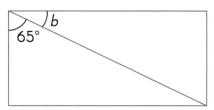

Measure of $\angle b$ = ⬚ °

Find the unknown measures of the angles in the square and rectangle.

 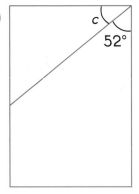

Measure of $\angle c$ = ☐ °

 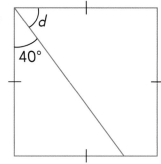

Measure of $\angle d$ = ☐ °

Learn **Use the properties of squares and rectangles to find the side lengths of figures.**

Figure *ABCDEF* is made up of two rectangles. Find *BC*.

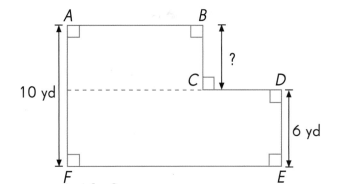

$BC = 10 - 6$
$\quad\ \ = 4$ yd

The opposite sides of a rectangle are of equal length.

Figure *GHIJKL* is made up of a square and a rectangle.
Find *IJ*.

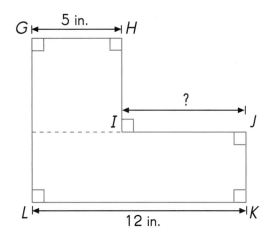

$IJ = 12 - 5$
$\quad\ = 7$ in.

The sides of a square are of equal length.

Guided Practice

Find the length of the unknown side in each figure.

5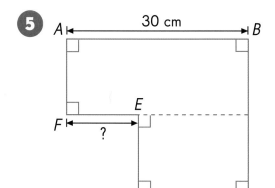

$FE =$ [   ] cm

6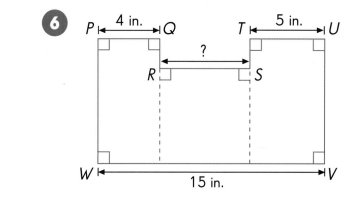

$RS =$ [   ] in.

All line segments in these figures meet at right angles.
Find the length of the unknown side in each figure.

7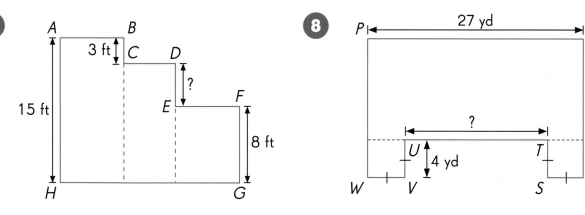

$DE =$ [   ] ft

8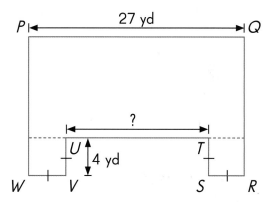

$UT =$ [   ] yd

 **Hands-On Activity**

WORK IN PAIRS

Material:
• centimeter grid paper

On grid paper, draw two different figures made up of squares and rectangles.

1 Find the perimeter of each figure.

2 Write the length of each side of the figures.

Example

The perimeter of each figure is 16 centimeters.

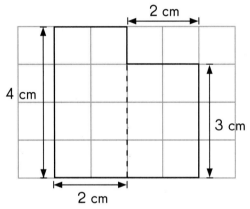

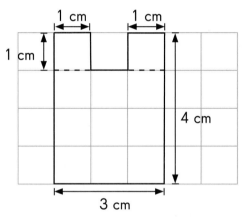

3 Draw more lines on each figure to form the smallest possible rectangle to enclose it.

4 Find the perimeter of each rectangle.

5 Compare the perimeter of each figure with the perimeter of the rectangle that encloses it.

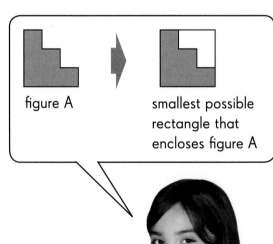

figure A

smallest possible rectangle that encloses figure A

Find the unknown measures of the angles in each square or rectangle.

1 *ABCD* is a square. Find the measure of ∠a.

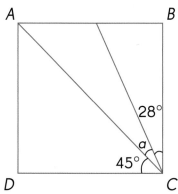

Measure of ∠a = [   ]°

2 *PQRS* is a rectangle. The measure of ∠PQS is 32° and the measure of ∠SPX is 48°. Find the measures of ∠a, ∠b, and ∠c.

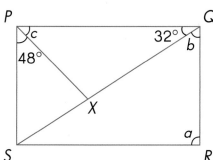

Measure of ∠a = [   ]°

Measure of ∠b = [   ]°

Measure of ∠c = [   ]°

All the line segments in these figures meet at right angles.
Find the lengths of the unknown sides in each figure.

3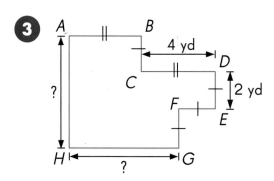

AH = [   ] yd

HG = [   ] yd

4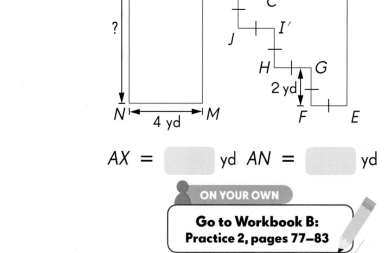

AX = [   ] yd AN = [   ] yd

ON YOUR OWN

Go to Workbook B:
Practice 2, pages 77–83

PROBLEM SOLVING

1 Find 8 sticks you must remove to leave behind 2 squares.

2 Use squares and rectangles of these sizes.

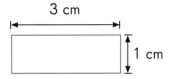

a How many of these squares and rectangles can you use to form a square with 3-centimeter sides?

b How many of these squares and rectangles can you use to form a rectangle with a length of 4 centimeters and a width of 3 centimeters?

ON YOUR OWN

Go to Workbook B:
Put on Your Thinking Cap!
pages 83–86

Chapter Wrap Up

Study Guide

You have learned...

Squares and Rectangles

Properties of Squares

- four sides of equal length
- opposite sides that are parallel
- four right angles
- a special type of rectangle

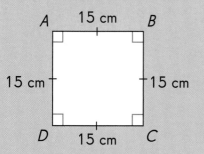

$\overline{AB} \parallel \overline{DC}$ and $\overline{AD} \parallel \overline{BC}$

Properties of Rectangles

- four sides
- opposite sides that are of equal length and parallel
- four right angles
- may or may not be a square

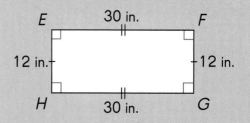

$\overline{EF} \parallel \overline{HG}$ and $\overline{FG} \parallel \overline{EH}$

Some figures are made up of squares and rectangles.

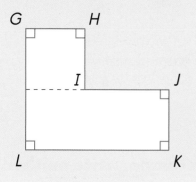

Find Unknown Measurements

Find side lengths and angle measures in squares and rectangles.

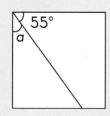

Measure of $\angle a$
$= 90° - 55°$
$= 35°$

Find lengths in figures made up of squares and rectangles.

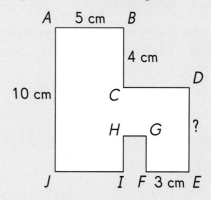

$DE = 10 - 4$
$\quad\quad = 6$ cm

Chapter Review/Test

Vocabulary

Choose the correct word.

square

rectangle

right angle

parallel

1 A four-sided figure with four right angles, and all sides of equal length is a ▭ .

2 A four-sided figure with opposite sides of equal length, and four right angles is a ▭ .

3 An angle that measures 90° is called a ▭ .

Concepts and Skills

Complete.

Figure *ABCD* is a square.

4 $AB =$ ▭ $=$ ▭ $=$ ▭

5 Measure of $\angle a =$ measure of $\angle$ ▭

$=$ measure of $\angle$ ▭ $=$ measure of $\angle$ ▭ $=$ ▭ °

Figure *EFGH* is a rectangle.

6 $EF =$ ▭

7 $EH =$ ▭

8 Measure of $\angle e =$ measure of $\angle$ ▭

$=$ measure of $\angle$ ▭ $=$ measure of $\angle$ ▭ $=$ ▭ °

Identify each figure. If it is neither a square nor a rectangle, write neither.

9 ▭

10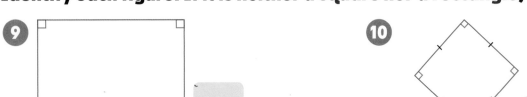

Identify each figure. If it is neither a **square** nor a **rectangle**, write **neither.**

11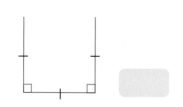

12

Solve.

13 *ABCD* is a square. Find the measures of ∠*b* and ∠*d*, and *AD*.

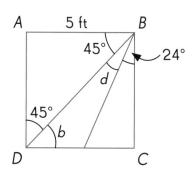

Measure of ∠*b* = [   ]°

Measure of ∠*d* = [   ]°

AD = [   ] ft

14 *WXYZ* is a rectangle. Find the measures of ∠*ZXY* and ∠*XWO*, and *YZ*.

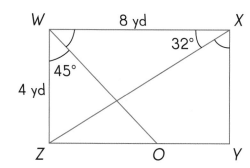

Measure of ∠*ZXY* = [   ]°

Measure of ∠*XWO* = [   ]°

YZ = [   ] yd

15 The figure is made up of a rectangle and a square.
Find *AH* and *FE*.

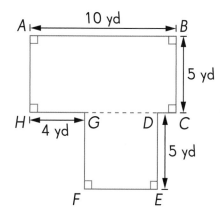

AH = [   ] yd

FE = [   ] yd

12 Area and Perimeter

Lessons

BIG IDEA

▶ Area and perimeter of a square, rectangle, or composite figure can be found by counting squares or using a formula.

Recall Prior Knowledge

Using an area model to show multiplication facts

There are 5 groups of 7 tomatoes.
How many tomatoes are there altogether?

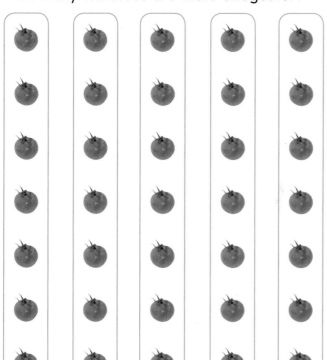

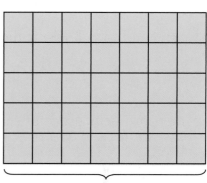

5 × 7

5 groups of 7
= 5 × 7
= 7 + 7 + 7 + 7 + 7
= 35

There are 35 tomatoes altogether.

Area

The area of a figure is the amount of surface covered by the figure.

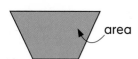
area

The standard units used for small areas are square centimeter (cm^2) and square inch (in.^{2}). The standard units used for large areas are square meter (m^2) and square foot (ft^2).

Finding the area of a figure

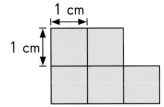

1 cm

1 cm

You can count square units to find the area.
The figure is made up of 5 one-centimeter squares.
The area of the figure is 5 square centimeters.

Perimeter

The perimeter of a figure is the distance around it.

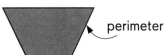

perimeter

The standard units used for short distances are centimeter (cm) and inch (in.).
The standard units used for long distances are meter (m) and foot (ft).

Finding the perimeter of a figure

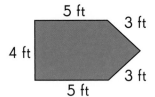

5 ft

3 ft

4 ft

3 ft

5 ft

You can add the lengths of sides to find the perimeter.
Perimeter = 5 + 3 + 3 + 5 + 4
= 20 ft
The perimeter of the figure is 20 feet.

✔ Quick Check

Multiply.

1 There are 3 boxes of 5 pencils in each box.
How many pencils are there in all?

$$3 \times 5 = \boxed{} \text{ rows of } \boxed{}$$

$$= \boxed{} + \boxed{} + \boxed{}$$

$$= \boxed{}$$

There are $\boxed{}$ pencils in all.

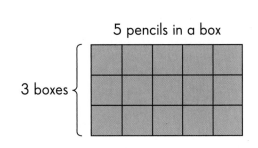

5 pencils in a box

3 boxes

Trace these figures. Outline the perimeter and shade the area of each figure.

2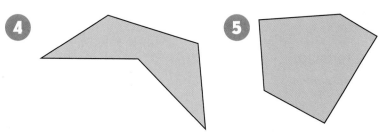

3

4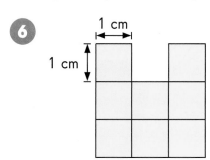

5

Find the area of the figure.
Each grid square is 1 square centimeter.

6

1 cm

1 cm

Area = ⬜ cm²

Find the perimeter of the figure.

7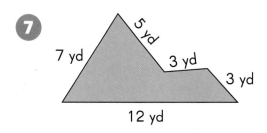

7 yd

5 yd

3 yd

3 yd

12 yd

Perimeter = ⬜ yd

Lesson 12.1 Area of a Rectangle

Lesson Objectives

- Estimate the area of a rectangle by counting grid squares.
- Find the area of a rectangle using a formula.

> **Vocabulary**
> length
> width

ᴸᵉᵃʳⁿ Find the area of a rectangle by counting squares.

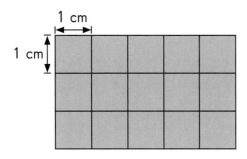

What is the area of the rectangle? Count the one-centimeter squares covering the rectangle to find out.

There are 3 rows of squares.
Each row has 5 squares.
There are 15 one-centimeter squares covering the rectangle.
So, the area of the rectangle is 15 square centimeters.

ᴸᵉᵃʳⁿ Find the area of a rectangle using a formula.

The longer side of the rectangle is usually called the **length**.
The shorter side is called the **width**.

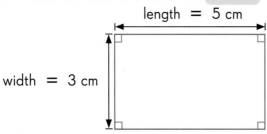

width = 3 cm

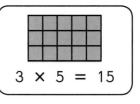

$3 \times 5 = 15$

> Area of rectangle = length × width

Area = 5 × 3
    = 15 cm^2

Square centimeters is abbreviated cm^2.

Guided Practice

Find the area of each rectangle.

1

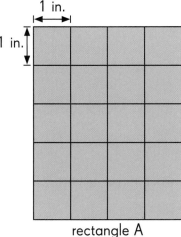

1 in.

1 in.

rectangle A

> Count the number of one-inch squares covering rectangle A.

There are [ ] rows of one-inch squares.

Each row has [ ] one-inch squares.

There are [ ] one-inch squares

covering rectangle A.

Area of rectangle A = [ ] in.²

2

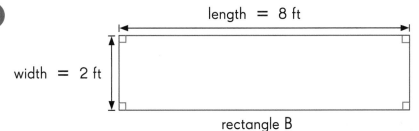

length = 8 ft

width = 2 ft

rectangle B

> What is the other way to find the area of a rectangle?

Area of rectangle B = length × width

= [ ] × [ ]

= [ ] ft²

Find the area of the square.

3 Square C is covered with one-meter squares.
Find the area of square C using two different methods.

Method 1

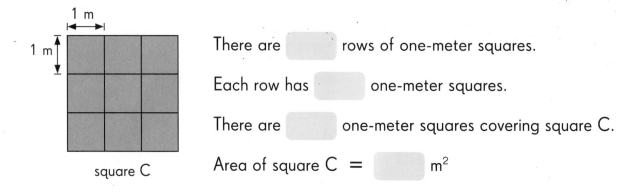

square C

There are [ ] rows of one-meter squares.

Each row has [ ] one-meter squares.

There are [ ] one-meter squares covering square C.

Area of square C = [ ] m²

Method 2

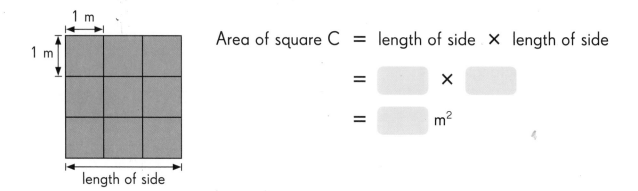

length of side

Area of square C = length of side × length of side

= [ ] × [ ]

= [ ] m²

The lengths of all sides of a square are equal.

Find the area of each figure.

4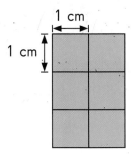

1 cm

1 cm

Area = length × width

= [ ] × [ ]

= [ ] cm²

5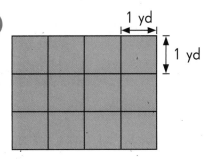

1 yd

1 yd

Area = length × width

= [ ] × [ ]

= [ ] yd²

Find the area of each rectangle or square.

6

7 in.

3 in.

Area = [ ] in.²

7

4 mi

4 mi

Area = [ ] mi²

8

9 ft

2 ft

Area = [ ] ft²

9

6 yd

6 yd

Area = [ ] yd²

  **Hands-On Activity**

Materials:
• geoboard
• rubber bands
• dot paper

WORKING TOGETHER

1 Work in groups of four.
Use a geoboard and rubber bands to make four rectangles.
Each rectangle should be a different size.
Each side should be parallel to the border of the geoboard.
Use dot paper to record your figures.

The squares formed by the pegs of a geoboard are square units.
For each rectangle,

a find the number of horizontal rows of square units.

b find the number of square units in each row.

c find the area using the formula.

Area = length × width

2 Use these line segments to make three rectangles of different sizes.
Use each line segment twice. Use dot paper to record your figures.
Find the perimeter and area of each rectangle.

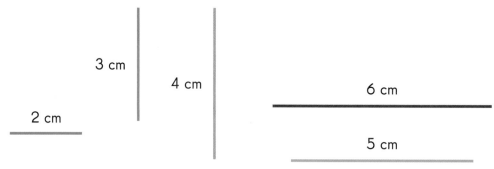

3 cm

4 cm

6 cm

2 cm

5 cm

7 cm

Guided Practice

Solve.

10 Janel bent a 36-inch wire to make a square photo frame. What is the area inside the photo frame?

Length of one side = ⬚ ÷ 4

= ⬚ in.

Area inside photo frame = ⬚ × ⬚

= ⬚ in.^{2}

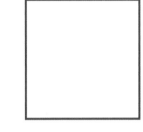

11 The length of one side of a square garden is 8 yards. Half of the garden was used for growing vegetables. What area of the garden was used for growing vegetables?

Method 1

Half of length of one side of square garden

= ⬚ ÷ 2

= ⬚ yd

Area of garden used for growing vegetables

= ⬚ × ⬚

= ⬚ yd^2

Method 2

Area of garden = ⬚ × 8

= ⬚ yd^2

Area of garden used for growing vegetables = ⬚ ÷ 2

= ⬚ yd^2

Estimate the area of a figure.

Use rounding to estimate the areas of the figures.

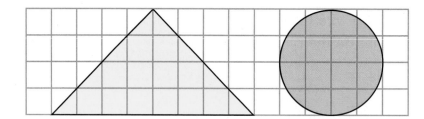

Shaded Region	Area of Shaded Region	Approximate Area
☐	1 square unit	1 square unit
◱	$\frac{1}{2}$ square unit	$\frac{1}{2}$ square unit
▨	greater than $\frac{1}{2}$ square unit	1 square unit
◻	less than $\frac{1}{2}$ square unit	0 square unit

Look at the triangle. Count the squares.

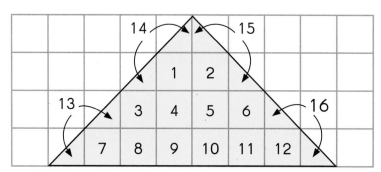

The area of the triangle is 16 square units.

Look at the circle. Count the squares.

The area of the circle is about 12 square units.

Guided Practice

Estimate the area of each figure. Count the square units.

Count 1 square unit.   Count $\frac{1}{2}$ square unit.   Count 1 square unit.   Count 0 square units.

12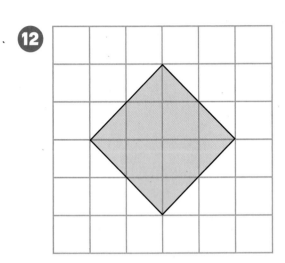

13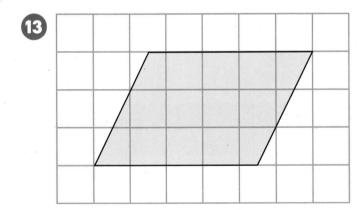

14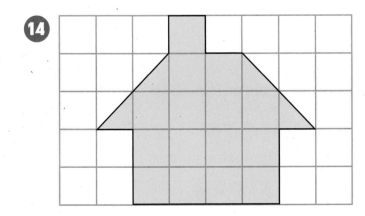

Hands-On Activity

Material:
• square grid paper

Do you know what the area of your palm is?
Place your palm on a square grid.
Trace the outline of your palm.
Count the squares to estimate the area of your palm.

 Count 1 square unit.

Count $\frac{1}{2}$ square unit.

 Count 1 square unit.

 Count 0 square units.

Let's Practice

Find the area of the figure.

1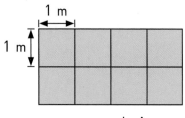

rectangle A

There are _____ rows of one-meter squares.

Each row has _____ one-meter squares.

There are _____ one-meter squares

covering rectangle A.

Area of rectangle A = _____ m^2

Find the area of the figure.

2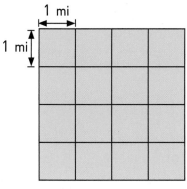

town B

Area of town B = length of side × length of side

= [ ] × [ ]

= [ ] mi²

Find the area of each rectangle or square.

3

6 in.

3 in.

Area = [ ] in.²

4

7 cm

7 cm

Area = [ ] cm²

Solve.

5 The length of one side of a square window is 24 inches.
Half of the window is covered with ivy.
What area of the window is covered with ivy?

Estimate the area of each shaded figure.

6

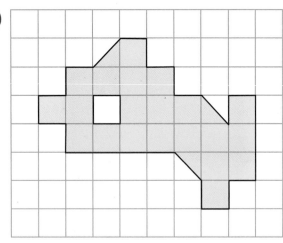

Use this to help you remember what you counted.

Number of =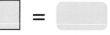

Number of =

Number of =

Number of =

The area of the figure is [ ] square units.

7

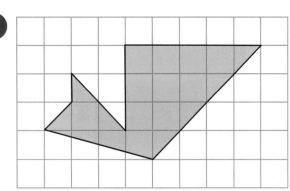

Use this to help you remember what you counted.

Number of =

Number of =

Number of =

Number of =

The area of the figure is [ ] square units.

ON YOUR OWN

Go to Workbook B:
Practice 1, pages 93–98

Lesson 12.2 Rectangles and Squares

Lesson Objective

- Solve problems involving the area and perimeter of squares and rectangles.

Find the perimeter of a rectangle using a formula.

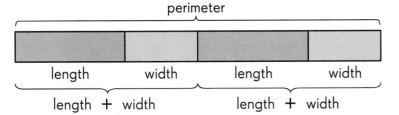

length

width

Perimeter of rectangle = length + width + length + width
= total length of all four sides

perimeter

| length | width | length | width |

length + width   length + width

So, the length + width of a rectangle is equal to $\frac{1}{2}$ of its perimeter.

> You can use a model to show that the perimeter of the rectangle is the sum of its two lengths and two widths.

Find one side of a rectangle given its perimeter and the other side.

The perimeter of rectangle A is 18 feet.
Its length is 6 feet. Find its width.

$$\begin{aligned} \text{Length} + \text{width} &= \text{perimeter} \div 2 \\ &= 18 \div 2 \\ &= 9 \text{ ft} \end{aligned}$$

$$\begin{aligned} \text{Length} + \text{width} &= 9 \text{ ft} \\ 6 + \text{width} &= 9 \text{ ft} \\ \text{width} &= 9 - 6 \\ &= 3 \text{ ft} \end{aligned}$$

The width of rectangle A is 3 feet.

6 ft

?

rectangle A

Guided Practice

Solve.

1 The perimeter of rectangle B is 28 yards.
Its length is 8 yards. Find its width.

Length + width = perimeter ÷ 2

= [   ] ÷ [   ]

= [   ] yd

8 + width = [   ] yd

width = [   ] − [   ]

= [   ] yd

The width of rectangle B is [   ] yards.

8 yd

?

rectangle B

2 The perimeter of a rectangular pool is 32 yards. Its width is 5 yards.
Find the length of the pool.

?

5 yd

Learn · Find one side of a square given its perimeter.

The perimeter of a square is 64 meters.
Find the length of a side of the square.

All the sides of a square are equal.
There are 4 sides in a square.

Length of a side = perimeter ÷ 4

= 64 ÷ 4

= 16 m

The length of a side of the square is 16 meters.

? m

Guided Practice

Solve.

3 Linda bent a wire 132 centimeters long into a square.
What is the length of a side of the square?

Length of a side = ⬚ ÷ 4

= ⬚ cm

The length of a side of the square is ⬚ centimeters.

4 The perimeter of a square gymnasium is 36 yards.

Find the length of one side of the gymnasium.

```
         ? yd
    ┌──────────┐
    │          │
    │          │
    │          │
    └──────────┘
```

Let's Practice

Solve.

1 The perimeter of a rectangular garden
is 128 feet. Its length is 35 feet.
Find the width of the garden.

```
        35 ft
    ┌──────────┐
    │          │
  ? │          │
    │          │
    └──────────┘
```

2 Jung glued a 72-centimeter piece of decorative
string around the outer edge of a square-topped box.
What is the length of one side of the square top?

3 Colin walked once around a rectangular field
for a total distance of 480 meters.
The length of the field is 160 meters.
What is the width of the field?

ON YOUR OWN

Go to Workbook B:
Practice 2, pages 99–102

^Le^{arn} **Find the area of a rectangle using a formula.**

Area of rectangle = length × width

In the rectangle, area = 5 × 3

$\qquad\qquad\qquad$ = 15 unit^2.

The area of the rectangle is 15 square units.

length

width

^Le^{arn} **Find one side of a rectangle given its area and the other side.**

The area of a rectangular carpet is 63 square meters.
Its length is 9 meters. Find its width.

$$\text{Length} \times \text{width} = \text{area}$$
$$9 \times \text{width} = 63 \text{ m}^2$$
$$\text{Width} = 63 \div 9$$
$$= 7 \text{ m}$$

The width of the rectangular carpet is 7 meters.

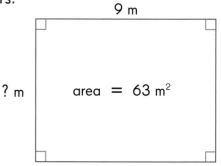

9 m

? m   area = 63 m^2

Guided Practice

Solve. Show your work.

5 The area of a rectangular piece of land is 96 square yards.
Its width is 8 yards. Find its length.

Length × ⬚ = ⬚ yd

$\qquad$ Length = ⬚ ÷ ⬚

$\qquad\qquad$ = ⬚ yd

The length of the rectangular piece of land is ⬚ yards.

Learn **Find one side and the perimeter of a square given its area.**

The area of square G is 25 square centimeters.

a Find the length of a side of the square.

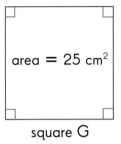

Area = length of side × length of side

25 = 5 × 5

Length of side = 5 cm

area = 25 cm²

square G

The length of a side of square G is 5 centimeters.

b Find the perimeter of the square.

Perimeter = 4 × length of side

= 4 × 5

= 20 cm

The perimeter of square G is 20 centimeters.

Guided Practice

Solve. Show your work.

6 The area of square H is 49 square inches.

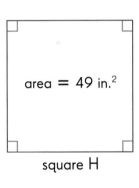

area = 49 in.²

square H

a Find the length of a side of the square.

Area = 49 in.²

49 = [   ] × [   ]

Length of side = [   ] in.

The length of a side of square H

is [   ] inches.

Use mental math to find a number that when multiplied by itself is 49.

b Find the perimeter of the square.

Perimeter = 4 × [   ]

= [   ] in.

The perimeter of square H is [   ] inches.

Let's Explore!

WORKING TOGETHER

Work in groups of four.
Use rubber bands to make as many different rectangles
as possible on the geoboard.
Make sure that all the rectangles you make have the same perimeter.
Use dot paper to record your figures.
Record the data about the rectangles in a table like the one below.

Example

Rectangle	Length	Width	Perimeter	Area
A	3 in.	3 in.	12 in.	9 in.^{2}
B	4 in.	2 in.	12 in.	8 in.^{2}

What do you notice about the area of these rectangles?

Let's Practice

Solve.

1 The area of a rectangular garden is 48 square meters. Its length is 8 meters. Find its width.

2 The area of a square plate is 81 square centimeters. Find the length of a side of the square plate.

? cm | area = 81 cm²

3 The area of a rectangular office is 108 square feet. Its width is 9 feet.

a Find its length.

b Find the perimeter of the office.

4 The area of a square kitchen is 16 square meters.

a Find the length of a side of the kitchen.

b Find the perimeter of the kitchen.

5 The perimeter of a square garden is 24 yards.

a Find the length of its side.

b Find the area of the garden.

6 The perimeter of a rectangular land preserve is 36 miles. Its length is twice the width.

a Find the length and width of the land preserve.

b Find the area of the land preserve.

ON YOUR OWN

Go to Workbook B: Practice 3, pages 103–106

12.3 Composite Figures

Lesson Objective

- Find the perimeter and area of a composite figure.

Learn **Find the perimeter of a composite figure by adding the lengths of its sides.**

A composite figure is made up of different shapes.

A homeowner wants to fence in this piece of land. He draws a diagram and labels it *ABCDEF*. Find *CD* and *AF*.

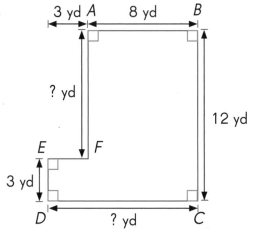

$CD = EF + AB$
$\quad\ = 3 + 8$
$\quad\ = 11$ yd

$AF = BC - DE$
$\quad\ = 12 - 3$
$\quad\ = 9$ yd

Perimeter of *ABCDEF* = *AB* + *BC* + *CD* + *DE* + *EF* + *AF*
$\qquad\qquad\qquad\qquad = 8 + 12 + 11 + 3 + 3 + 9$
$\qquad\qquad\qquad\qquad = 46$ yd

The perimeter of *ABCDEF* is 46 yards.

Guided Practice

Solve. Show your work.

1 Find the perimeter of figure *ABCDEF*.

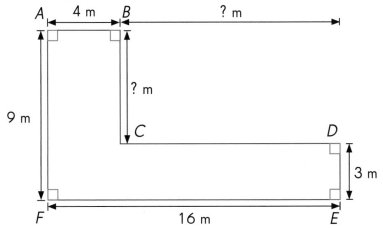

First, find *BC* and *CD*.

$BC = AF - DE$

$= \boxed{} - \boxed{}$

$= \boxed{}$ m

$CD = \boxed{} - \boxed{}$

$= \boxed{} - \boxed{}$

$= \boxed{}$ m

Perimeter of figure *ABCDEF*

$= AB + \boxed{} + \boxed{} + \boxed{} + \boxed{} + \boxed{}$

$= \boxed{} + \boxed{} + \boxed{} + \boxed{} + \boxed{} + \boxed{}$

$= \boxed{}$ m

Find the perimeter of each figure.

2

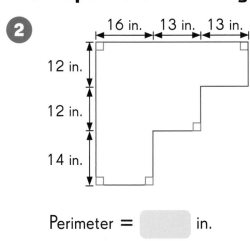

Perimeter = $\boxed{}$ in.

3

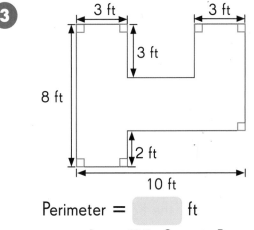

Perimeter = $\boxed{}$ ft

Learn **Find the area of a composite figure by adding the area of its parts.**

Find the area of the figure.

This figure is made up of two rectangles.
It is a composite figure.

Area of a rectangle = length × width
Area of rectangle A = 8 × 4 = 32 cm²
Area of rectangle B = 10 × 3 = 30 cm²
Area of the figure   = area of rectangle A + area of rectangle B
                                 = 32 + 30
                                 = 62 cm²

The area of the figure is 62 square centimeters.

Guided Practice

Solve.

4 Find the area of the figure.
It is made up of a square and a rectangle.

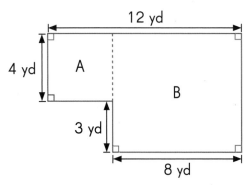

You can also divide the figure into two rectangles like this.

How do you find the area now?

Area of square A   = ▢ × ▢

                               = ▢ yd²

Area of rectangle B = ▢ × ▢

                               = ▢ yd²

Area of the figure   = ▢ + ▢ = ▢ yd²

The area of the figure is ▢ square yards.

Find the area of each figure.

5

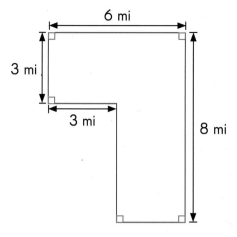

Area = [ ] mi²

6

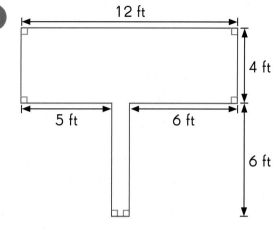

Area = [ ] ft²

7

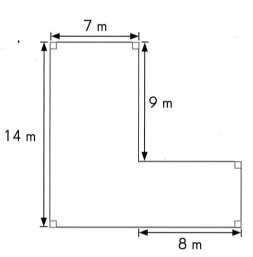

Area = [ ] m²

8

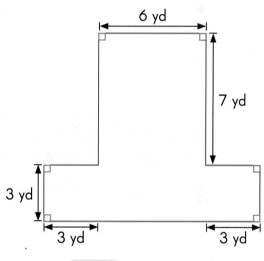

Area = [ ] yd²

9

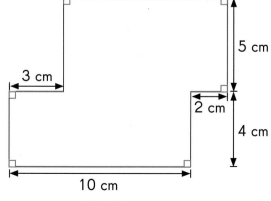

Area = [ ] cm²

Hands-On Activity

Materials:
• square grid paper
• scissors

WORK IN PAIRS

STEP
1 Draw two rectangles on a sheet of square grid paper and cut them out.

STEP
2 Draw one rectangle and one square on another sheet of square grid paper and cut them out.

STEP
3 Draw two rectangles and one square on a third sheet of square grid paper and cut them out.

STEP
4 Form as many different composite figures as you can using each set of cutouts.

Example

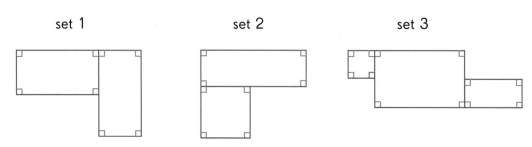

set 1   set 2   set 3

STEP
5 Draw the figures formed on another sheet of square grid paper. Compare your figures with those of your classmates.

STEP
6 Find the perimeter and area of each figure you have formed.

You may also use a computer tool to draw and combine squares and rectangles.

Tech Connection

Find the perimeter and area of each composite figure.

1

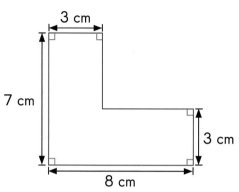

Perimeter = ⬚ cm

Area = ⬚ cm²

2

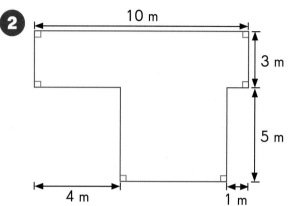

Perimeter = ⬚ m

Area = ⬚ m²

3

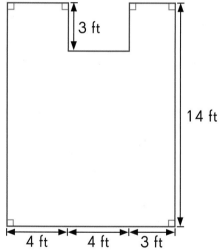

Perimeter = ⬚ ft

Area = ⬚ ft²

4

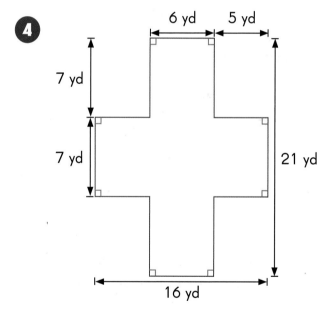

Perimeter = ⬚ yd

Area = ⬚ yd²

ON YOUR OWN

Go to Workbook B:
Practice 4, pages 107–110

 12.4 Using Formulas for Area and Perimeter

Lesson Objectives

• Solve word problems involving estimating area of figures.
• Solve word problems involving area and perimeter of composite figures.

Learn Use length and width to find the area of a rectangle.

Randy bought a diary for his brother.
What is the area of its cover page?

Randy can find the area by measuring the length and width of the cover page.

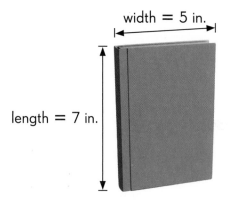

width = 5 in.

length = 7 in.

Step 1 Length of cover page = 7 in.

Step 2 Width of cover page = 5 in.

Step 3 Area of cover page = length ✕ width
                                  = 7 ✕ 5
                                  = 35 in.^{2}

The area of the cover page is 35 square inches.

Use squares to estimate the area of a figure.

Twyla is building a model of a park.
She wants to know how large the model of the pond is.

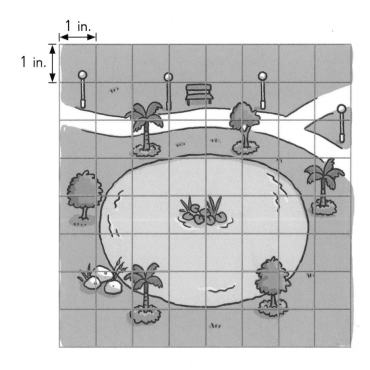

1 in.

1 in.

Help her estimate the area of the model.

| | Count 1 square unit. | | Count $\frac{1}{2}$ square unit. | | Count 1 square unit. | | Count 0 square units. |

Step 1 Count the ☐.
There are 10 ☐.

Step 2 Count the ◺.
There are no ◺.

Step 3 Count the ◲.
There are 10 ◲.

Step 4 Add the squares.
10 + 10 = 20

The area of the model of the pond is about 20 square inches.

Guided Practice

Solve.

1 Find the area of the photo frame.

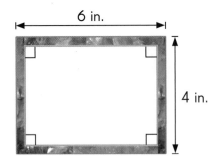

6 in.

4 in.

Area = ☐ in.²

2 Estimate the area of the CD.

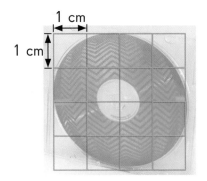

1 cm

1 cm

Estimated area = ☐ cm²

Learn **Use subtraction to find the area of a composite figure.**

The figure shows a small rectangle *BCDG* and a large rectangle *ACEF*.
Find the area of the shaded part of the figure.

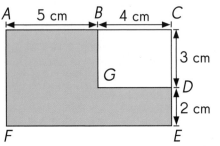

A   5 cm   B   4 cm   C

3 cm

G

D

2 cm

F   E

Area of shaded part
= area of large rectangle − area of small rectangle

Length of large rectangle = *AC*
$$= 5 + 4 = 9 \text{ cm}$$
Width of large rectangle = *CE*
$$= 3 + 2 = 5 \text{ cm}$$
Area of large rectangle $= 9 \times 5$
$$= 45 \text{ cm}^2$$
Area of small rectangle $= 4 \times 3$
$$= 12 \text{ cm}^2$$
Area of shaded part $= 45 - 12$
$$= 33 \text{ cm}^2$$

The area of the shaded part is 33 square centimeters.

Guided Practice

Solve. Show your work.

3 The figure shows a small rectangle *BCGH* and a large rectangle *ADEF*. Find the area of the shaded part of the figure.

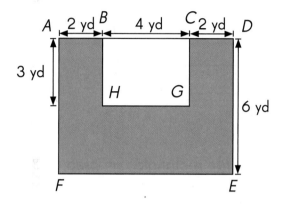

Length of large rectangle = [ ] + [ ] + [ ]

= [ ] yd

Width of large rectangle = [ ] yd

Area of large rectangle = [ ] × [ ]

= [ ] yd²

Area of small rectangle = [ ] × [ ]

= [ ] yd²

Area of shaded part = [ ] − [ ]

= [ ] yd²

First, find the area of the large rectangle.

The area of the shaded part is 36 square yards.

Learn **Find the area of a path around a rectangle.**

The figure shows a rectangular field with a path 2 meters wide around it.
Find the area of the path.

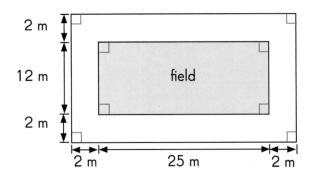

Area of path = area of large rectangle — area of small rectangle

Length of large rectangle = 2 + 25 + 2
                           = 29 m
Width of large rectangle = 2 + 12 + 2
                          = 16 m
Area of large rectangle = 29 × 16
                         = 464 m^2
Area of small rectangle = 25 × 12
                         = 300 m^2
Area of path   = 464 − 300
                         = 164 m^2

The area of the path is 164 square meters.

Guided Practice

Solve. Show your work.

4 A rectangular piece of fabric measures 80 inches by 60 inches.
When placed on a table, it leaves a margin 5 inches wide all around it.
Find the area of the table not covered by the fabric.

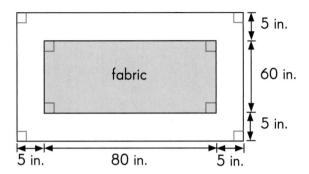

Area of table not covered by fabric = area of table − area of fabric

Length of table = [　] + [　] + [　]

= [　] in.

Width of table = [　] + [　] + [　]

= [　] in.

Area of table = [　] × [　]

= [　] in.²

Area of fabric = [　] × [　]

= [　] in.²

Area of table not covered by fabric = [　] − [　]

= [　] in.²

The area of the table not covered by the fabric is [　] square inches.

Solve.

5 Ryan has a rectangular sheet of paper with a length of 13 centimeters and a width of 8 centimeters. He cuts away a small rectangle at one of its corners. The length and width of the small rectangle are shown in the figure.

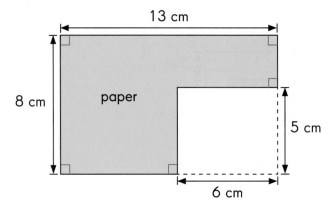

a Find the remaining area of the paper.

b Find the perimeter of the remaining paper.

6 There is a 1.5-yard wide path around a rectangular piece of land. The length and width of the path are shown in the figure.

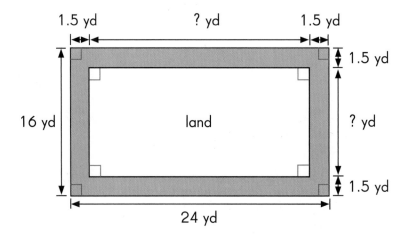

a Find the area of the land.

b Find the perimeter of the land.

Learn Find the area and perimeter of parts of a figure.

A corner of a square piece of paper is folded.

(a) Find the area of the shaded part.

The shaded part is half of a 2-inch square.

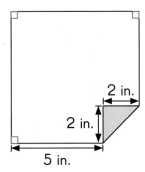

Area of 2-inch square = 2 × 2
= 4 in.²

So, area of shaded part = 4 ÷ 2
= 2 in.².

The area of the shaded part is 2 square inches.

(b) Find the perimeter of the square piece of paper unfolded.

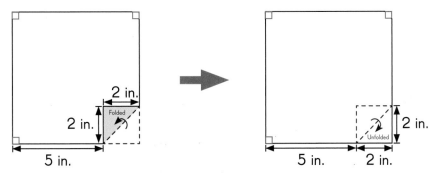

To find the perimeter of the square piece of paper unfolded, you need to find the length of a side of the square.

Length of a side = 5 + 2
= 7 in.

Perimeter of the square = 4 × 7
= 28 in.

The perimeter of the square piece of paper is 28 inches.

Guided Practice

Solve.

7 A rectangular piece of paper is folded at one of its corners so that the side *BC* lies along the side *CD* as shown.

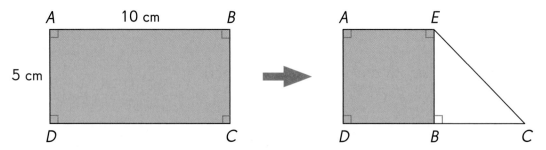

ⓐ Find the area of the rectangular piece of paper before it was folded.

ⓑ Find the area of the figure after the paper was folded.

 Hands-On Activity

Material:
• centimeter square grid paper

STEP
1 Draw a shape like this on square grid paper.

STEP
2 Estimate the area of the shape.

STEP
3 Draw the largest possible rectangle within the shape along the grid lines. Use the square grid to help you.

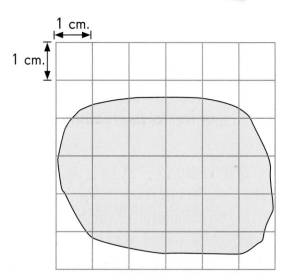

Let's Explore!

Material:
• centimeter square grid paper

STEP 1 Draw a rectangle with a length of 8 centimeters and a width of 6 centimeters on the centimeter grid paper.

STEP 2 Label the length and width. Find the area.

STEP 3 Cut out the rectangle.

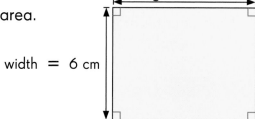

length = 8 cm

width = 6 cm

STEP 4 Fold the cut-out rectangle to make a rectangle of a different size. Measure the length and width of this shape. Then, find the area.

Example

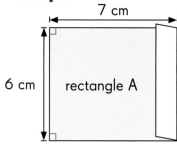

7 cm

6 cm

rectangle A

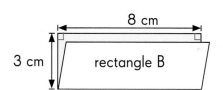

8 cm

3 cm

rectangle B

STEP 5 Unfold the rectangle you made in **STEP 4**. Fold it to make another rectangular shape. This time take only one measurement — measure the side that is changed by the folding. Then, find the area of the folded rectangle.

STEP 6 Check your answer by measuring the length and width of the folded rectangle.

STEP 7 Make two more rectangles with the cutout. Take only one measurement for each rectangle as in **STEP 5**.

Then, find its area. Does your method of using one measurement to find the area apply for these rectangles too?

Let's Practice

Solve.

1 The perimeter of a rectangular garden is 60 feet.
The width of a picket fence around the garden is 12 feet.
Find its length.

2 The filled figure is made up of 2-inch squares. Find the shaded area.

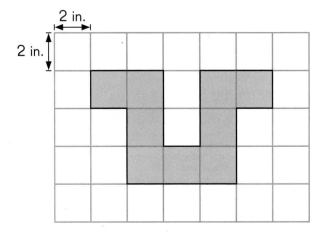

3 Cory spilled purple paint all over his grid paper.
Estimate the area covered by the paint.

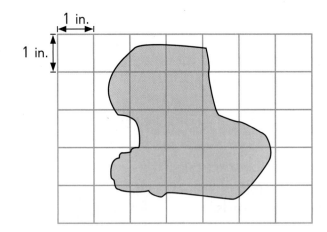

Solve.

4 The area below shows the cattleyard of a farmer.
Find the perimeter of the cattle fence around it.

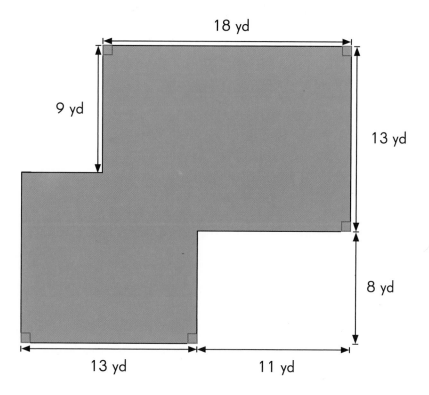

5 Lionel is laying a carpet on the floor of a rectangular room.
The border around the carpet is 1 meter wide.
How much space is not covered by the carpet?

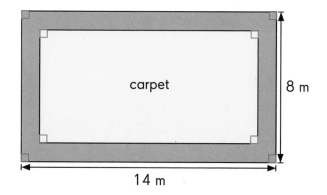

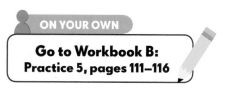

ON YOUR OWN

Go to Workbook B:
Practice 5, pages 111–116

Math Journal

1. The perimeter and length of a rectangle are given. List the steps to find the width.

2. The area of a square is given. Alice says that to find the length of one side, she can divide the area by 4. Is Alice correct? If not, explain to Alice how to find the length of one side of the square.

CRITICAL THINKING SKILLS

Put On Your Thinking Cap!

PROBLEM SOLVING

1. What is the length of one side of a square if its perimeter and area have the same numerical value?

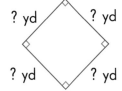

Make an organized list.

2. A rectangular piece of paper has a length of 12 inches and a width of 8 inches. What is the greatest number of 3-inch by 3-inch squares that can be drawn on the piece of paper, without overlapping?

CRITICAL THINKING SKILLS
Put On Your Thinking Cap!

PROBLEM SOLVING

3 Study the figure. All line segments meet at right angles.
What is the perimeter of the figure? Explain your reasoning.

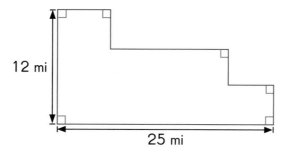

12 mi

25 mi

4 Vicky arranged two different square pieces of paper as shown.
The length of one side of each square piece of paper is a whole number.

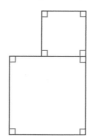

The total area of the figure is 89 square centimeters.
What is the length of the side of each square piece of paper?
On a piece of paper, copy and complete the table below.

Length of the Square (cm)	1	2	3	4	5	6	7	8	9	10
Area of the Square (cm²)	1	4	9							

Use the data in the table to find the areas of the two squares
that have a sum of 89 square centimeters.

ON YOUR OWN

Go to Workbook B:
Put on Your Thinking Cap!
pages 117–122

Chapter Wrap Up

Study Guide

You have learned...

BIG IDEA

▶ Area and perimeter of a square, rectangle, or composite figure can be found by counting squares or using a formula.

Perimeter

Area

Distance Around a Figure

Find the perimeter of a rectangle or square.
• Length + width + length + width
Use these units: cm, m, in., ft, yd, mi

Amount of Surface Covered

Find the area of a rectangle or square.
• Counting unit squares
• Length × width
Use these units: cm^2, m^2, $in.^2$, ft^2, yd^2, mi^2

Find the length of one side of a rectangle given the perimeter and the other side.

Length + width
= perimeter ÷ 2

Find the length of one side of a square given the perimeter.

Length of one side = perimeter ÷ 4

Find the area of a rectangle using the formula.

Length × width = area

Find the length of the sides of a square given the area.

Length of side × length of side = area

Find the length of one side of a rectangle given the area and the other side.

Length = area ÷ width

Composite Figures

Find Area

Divide the composite figure into rectangle(s) and/or square(s) to find the area.

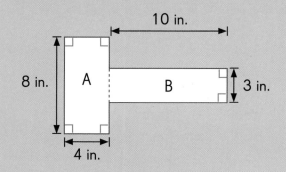

Area of rectangle A = 8 × 4
= 32 in.^{2}
Area of rectangle B = 10 × 3
= 30 in.^{2}
Area of figure = 32 + 30
= 62 in.^{2}

Find Perimeter

First, find the unknown lengths. Then find the perimeter.

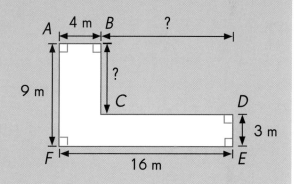

Perimeter
= 9 + 4 + 6 + 12 + 3 + 16
= 50 m

Chapter Review/Test

Vocabulary

Choose the correct word.

composite figure

length

width

1 The longer side of a rectangle is usually called

its [   ] and the shorter side is called its [   ] .

2 A figure made up of squares and rectangles is an example of

a [   ] .

Concepts and Skills

Find the missing lengths of the sides of each figure.

3

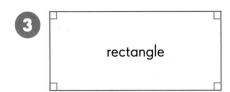

rectangle

Perimeter = 32 in.
Width   = 5 in.
Length   = [   ] in.

4

rectangle

Area   = 96 m²
Width = 8 m
Length = [   ] m

5

square

Perimeter = 28 yd
Length of one side = [   ] yd

6

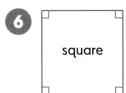

square

Area = 49 km²
Length of one side = [   ] km

7 **Find the area and perimeter of the figure.**

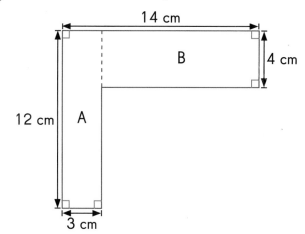

Area = [   ] cm²

Perimeter = [   ] cm

Problem Solving

Estimate the area of each figure.

8

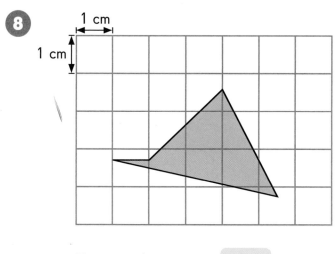

Estimated area = [   ]

9

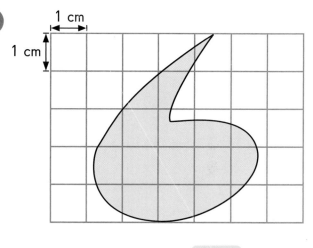

Estimated area = [   ]

Solve.

10 The figure shows a rectangular grass plot of land with a path through its center.

a How much land is covered with grass?

b How much fencing is needed to surround the land covered with grass?

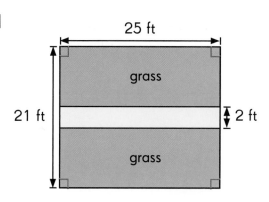

13 Symmetry

Symmetry in Nature

butterfly

scallop shell

starfish

crab

Lessons

BIG IDEA

▶ Figures can have line or rotational symmetry, or both.

Recall Prior Knowledge

Knowing polygons

A polygon is a closed figure formed from line segments
that meet only at their endpoints. These figures are polygons.

Identifying congruent figures

Shapes A and D have the same size and shape.
They are congruent.
Shapes B, C, and E are not congruent.

   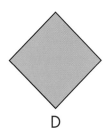 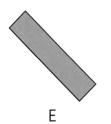

A	B	C	D	E

Identifying symmetric figures

Figures A and B are symmetric.
When figures A and B are folded along the dotted lines, the two halves
match exactly. Figures C and D are not symmetric.

 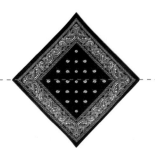 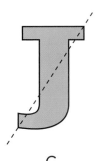 

A	B	C	D

Decide which of these figures are not polygons.

1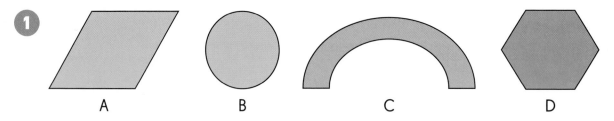

A   B   C   D

Decide which of these pairs of shapes are congruent.

2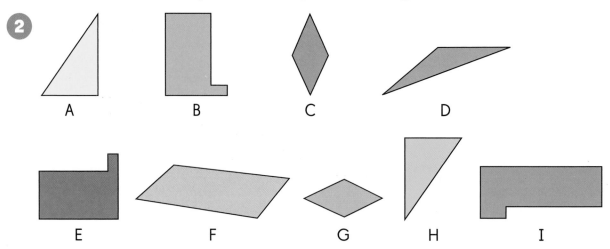

A   B   C   D

E   F   G   H   I

Identify the symmetric figures.

3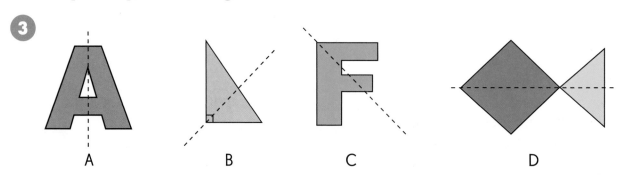

A   B   C   D

Lesson 13.1 Identifying Lines of Symmetry

Lesson Objective

* Identify a line of symmetry of a figure.

Vocabulary
line of symmetry
symmetric figure

ᴸᵉᵃʳⁿ Identify a line of symmetry of a figure.

Fold figure A along the dotted line as shown.

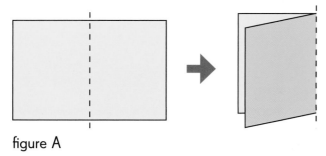

figure A

The two parts are congruent and they match exactly.
The dotted line is a **line of symmetry** of figure A.
So, figure A is a **symmetric figure** as it has line symmetry.

Now fold figure A along the dotted line as shown.

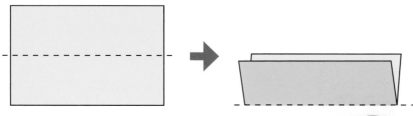

figure A

The two parts are congruent and they match exactly.
The dotted line is another line of symmetry of figure A.

A symmetric figure can have more than one line of symmetry.

Continued on next page

Now fold figure A along the line as shown.

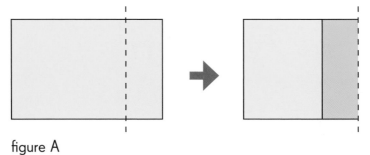

figure A

The two parts are not congruent so they do not match exactly.
The dotted line is not a line of symmetry.

Look at the two parts formed by folding along the dotted line.

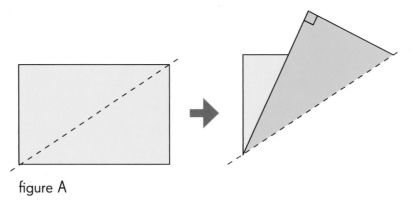

figure A

The two parts are congruent but they do not match exactly.
The dotted line is not a line of symmetry of figure A.

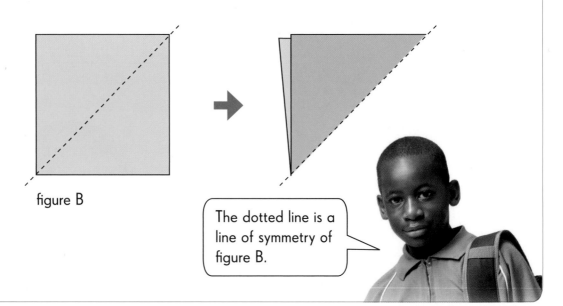

figure B

The dotted line is a line of symmetry of figure B.

Hands-On Activity

Materials:
• paper
• scissors

STEP
1 Fold a piece of paper in half.

STEP
2 Cut out a figure that starts from a point on the fold line and ends on another point on the same fold line.

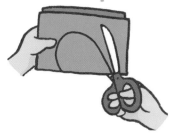

STEP
3 Unfold your symmetric figure.

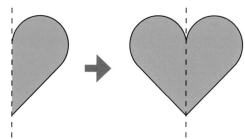

The fold line is a line of symmetry.

STEP
4 Compare your figure with those of your classmates.

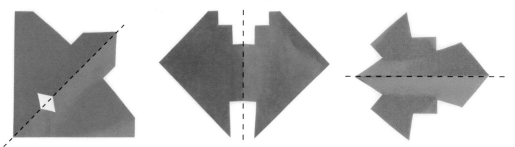

Guided Practice

Complete.

1 The dotted line divides each figure into two congruent parts.

Which of the dotted lines are lines of symmetry of each hexagon?

Remember to trace the dotted lines, too.

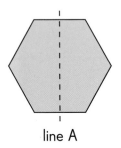

line A

Fold the hexagon along line A.

The two parts _____ exactly.

Line A is a _____ .

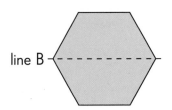

line B

Fold the hexagon along line B.

The two parts _____ exactly.

Line B is a _____ .

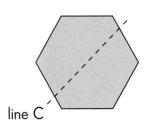

line C

Fold the hexagon along line C.

The two parts _____ exactly.

Line C is _____ .

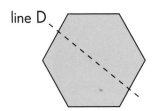

line D

Fold the hexagon along line D.

The two parts _____ exactly.

Line D is _____ .

Hands-On Activity

Materials:
- paper
- scissors
- coloring pencils

1 Use a sheet of paper with this shape on it.

STEP **1** Cut out the shape.

STEP **2** Fold the shape to get

a two parts that are congruent and match exactly.
Use a red coloring pencil to draw along the fold line.

b two parts that are congruent but do **not** match exactly.
Use a blue coloring pencil to draw along the fold line.

c two parts that are **not** congruent and do **not** match exactly.
Use a green coloring pencil to draw along the fold line.

Which of these lines is a line of symmetry? Explain your answer.

2 Use a computer drawing tool to draw these figures.

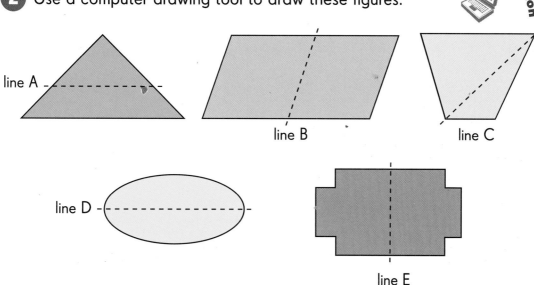

Print the figures and cut them out.
Draw a dotted line on each figure as shown and fold along it.
Which of the dotted lines are lines of symmetry?

Which of the dotted lines are lines of symmetry?

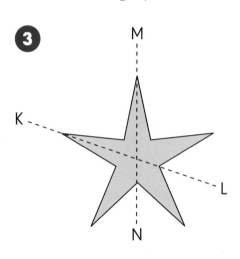

1

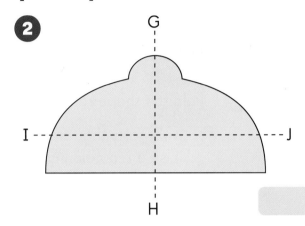

2

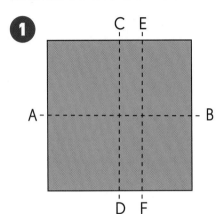

3

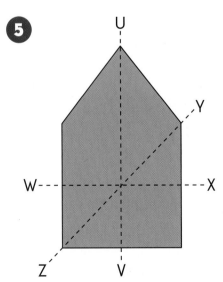

4

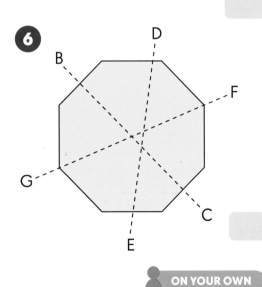

5

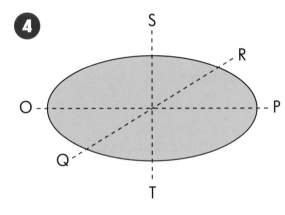

6

ON YOUR OWN

Go to Workbook B:
Practice 1, pages 123–124

13.2 Rotational Symmetry

Lesson Objectives

- Relate rotational symmetry to turns.
- Trace a figure to determine whether it has rotational symmetry.

Vocabulary

rotation

center of rotation

counter-clockwise

rotational symmetry

clockwise

Learn **A rotation turns a figure about a point.**

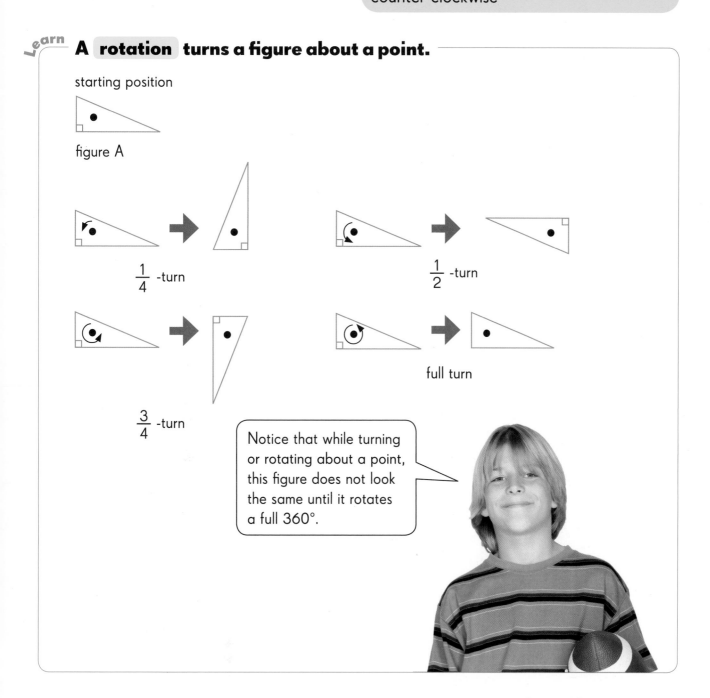

starting position

figure A

$\frac{1}{4}$ -turn

$\frac{1}{2}$ -turn

$\frac{3}{4}$ -turn

full turn

Notice that while turning or rotating about a point, this figure does not look the same until it rotates a full 360°.

Look at figure B.

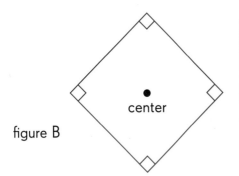

figure B

Clockwise: A rotation in the same direction as the hands on a clock.

Counter-clockwise: A rotation in the opposite direction as the hands on a clock.

Figure B was rotated counter-clockwise about its **center of rotation** through a

ⓐ $\frac{1}{4}$ -turn (90°):

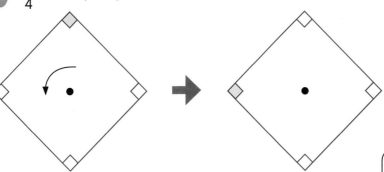

ⓑ $\frac{1}{2}$ -turn (180°):

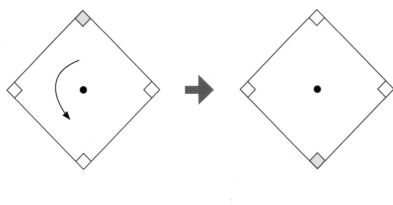

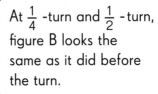

At $\frac{1}{4}$ -turn and $\frac{1}{2}$ -turn, figure B looks the same as it did before the turn.

c $\frac{3}{4}$ -turn (270°):

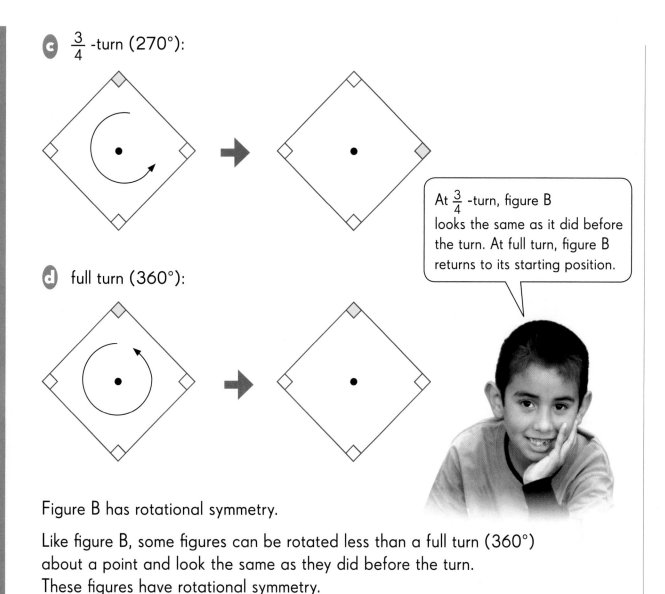

At $\frac{3}{4}$ -turn, figure B looks the same as it did before the turn. At full turn, figure B returns to its starting position.

d full turn (360°):

Figure B has rotational symmetry.

Like figure B, some figures can be rotated less than a full turn (360°) about a point and look the same as they did before the turn. These figures have rotational symmetry.

Guided Practice

Decide whether the figure has rotational symmetry. Explain your answer.

1 Figure A

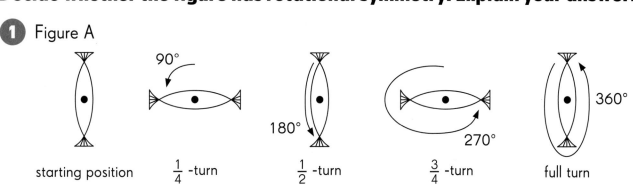

starting position $\frac{1}{4}$ -turn $\frac{1}{2}$ -turn $\frac{3}{4}$ -turn   full turn

Decide whether the figure has rotational symmetry. Explain your answer.

 Figure B

   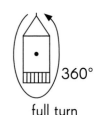

starting position $\frac{1}{4}$ -turn $\frac{1}{2}$ -turn $\frac{3}{4}$ -turn   full turn

Decide which figures have rotational symmetry. Explain your answer. Trace each figure to check.

  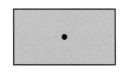 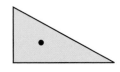

Hands-On Activity

Materials:
• grid paper
• pencil

WORK IN PAIRS

STEP **1** Draw one of these shapes on grid paper.

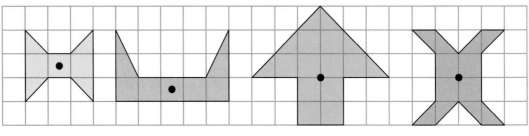

figure A   figure B   figure C   figure D

STEP **2** Your partner traces your drawing on another piece of grid paper, places a pencil tip in the center of the figure, and rotates it.

STEP **3** Decide whether the figure has rotational symmetry.

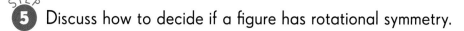

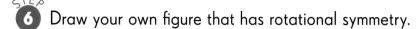

STEP
4 Switch roles and repeat STEP **1** to STEP **3** for the other three shapes.

STEP
5 Discuss how to decide if a figure has rotational symmetry.

STEP
6 Draw your own figure that has rotational symmetry.

Let's Practice

Decide if these figures have rotational symmetry. Use yes or no.

1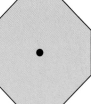

2

3

4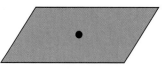

5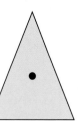

6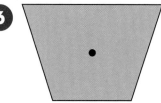

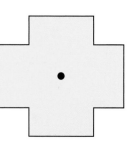

ON YOUR OWN

**Go to Workbook B:
Practice 2, pages 125–126**

Making Symmetric Shapes and Patterns

Lesson Objectives

- Draw a shape or pattern about a line of symmetry and check for rotational symmetry.
- Complete a symmetric shape or pattern.
- Create symmetric patterns on grid paper.

Learn **Form a symmetric pattern with rotational symmetry.**

Kelly created her own symmetric pattern on grid paper.

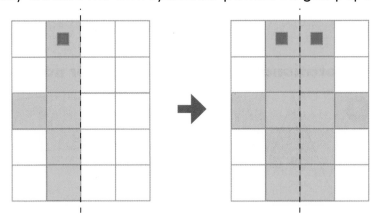

Kelly rotated the pattern through a $\frac{1}{2}$-turn (180°) about a point.
She found out that her pattern also had rotational symmetry.

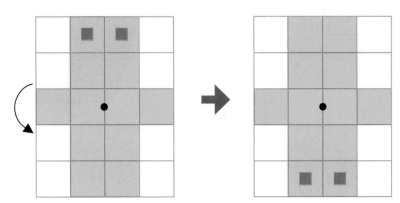

Guided Practice

Each figure shows half of a symmetric shape. The dotted line is a line of symmetry. Copy each figure on grid paper. Complete each symmetric shape. Decide which of these shapes have rotational symmetry.

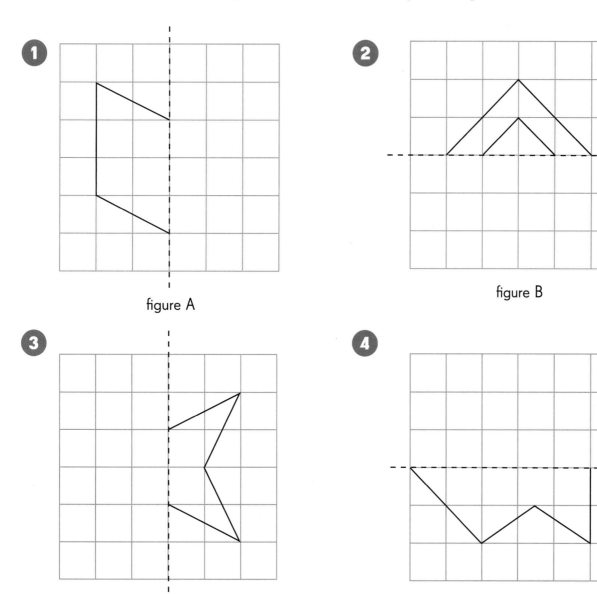

figure A

figure B

figure C

figure D

Each figure shows half of a symmetric pattern. The dotted line is a line of symmetry. Copy each figure on grid paper. Shade the squares to form a symmetric pattern about the given line of symmetry. Decide which of these figures have rotational symmetry.

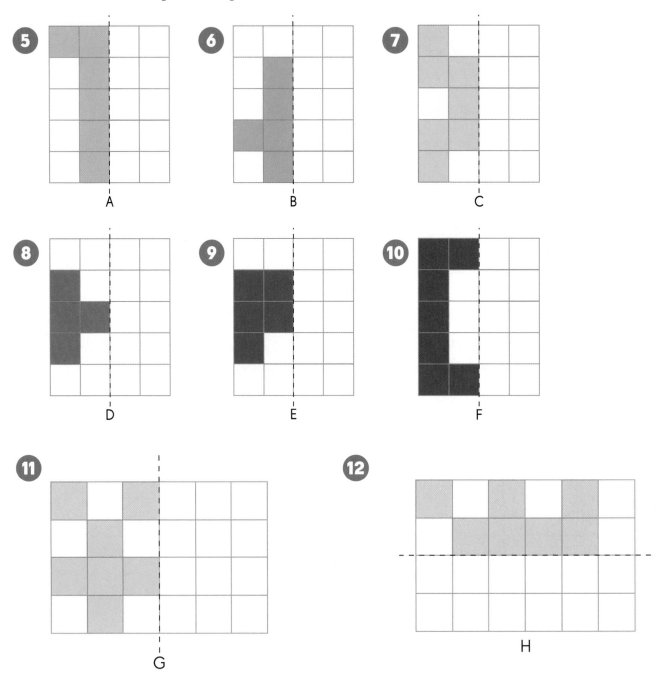

5   A

6   B

7   C

8   D

9   E

10   F

11   G

12   H

 **Hands-On Activity**

Materials:
• coloring pencil
• grid paper

STEP
1 Divide the grid paper into halves by drawing a dotted line as shown.

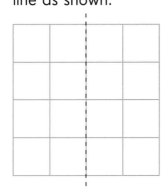

STEP
2 Color a square on the left side of the grid paper.

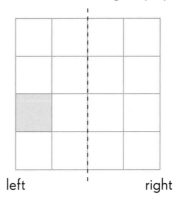

left   right

STEP
3 Color a square on the right side of the grid paper to form a symmetric pattern.

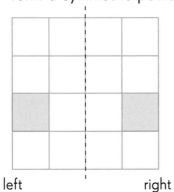

left   right

STEP
4 Continue coloring the left side, and then the right side until you have designed your own symmetric pattern. You may color ▢ or ◺.

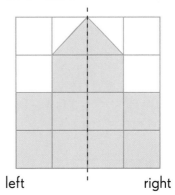

left   right

Let's Practice

Each figure shows half of a symmetric shape or pattern. The dotted line is a line of symmetry. Copy each figure on grid paper and complete it. Decide which of these figures have rotational symmetry. Use ✔ or ✗.

1
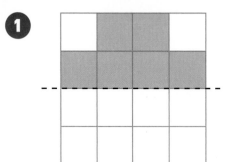

Rotational symmetry:

2
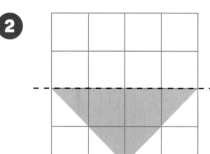

Rotational symmetry:

3
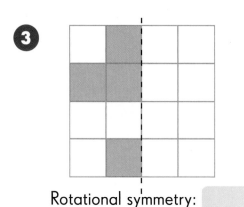

Rotational symmetry:

4
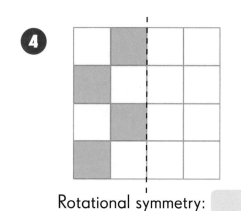

Rotational symmetry:

5

Rotational symmetry:

6
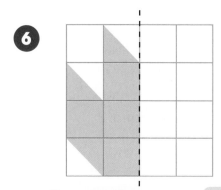

Rotational symmetry:

ON YOUR OWN

**Go to Workbook B:
Practice 3, pages 127–130**

CRITICAL THINKING SKILLS
Put On Your Thinking Cap!

PROBLEM SOLVING

1 Which of these figures are symmetric?

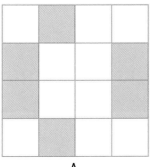

A

B

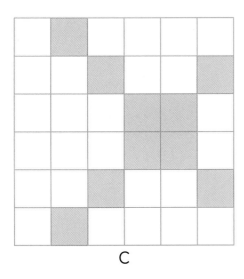

C

2 Which figure in Exercise 1 is not symmetric?
On a sheet of grid paper, copy the figure and color
one or more squares to make it symmetric.
Does it have rotational symmetry as well?

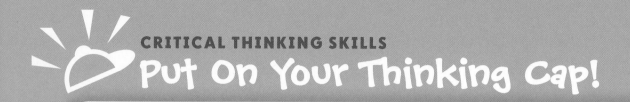

Put On Your Thinking Cap!

PROBLEM SOLVING

3 Lionel is making a pattern of symmetric figures. He has made three pieces of the pattern. Can you help Lionel to make the fourth piece? Draw it on a sheet of grid paper.

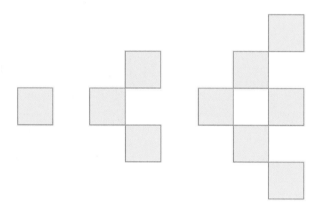

1st   2nd   3rd

ON YOUR OWN

Go to Workbook B:
Put on Your Thinking Cap!
pages 131–132

Chapter Wrap Up

Study Guide

You have learned...

Symmetry

Line Symmetry

To determine whether a given line is a line of symmetry of a figure.

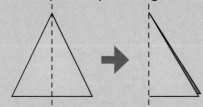

The two parts are congruent and they match exactly. So, the fold line is along a line of symmetry.

To recognize that a figure can have more than one line of symmetry.

Rotational Symmetry

To identify a figure which has rotational symmetry about a given point. Figures can be rotated clockwise or counter-clockwise about a center of rotation.

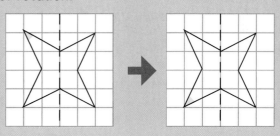

Making Symmetric Shapes and Patterns

To complete a symmetric shape or pattern given a line of symmetry, and half of the shape or pattern. Then to check it for rotational symmetry.

Symmetric shape

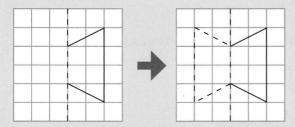

Symmetric pattern

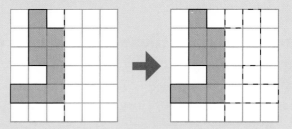

To create symmetric patterns on grid paper.

Chapter Review/Test

Vocabulary

Choose the correct word.

1 When a figure can be folded in half so that the two parts are congruent and match exactly, the figure has ▢ .

2 A line that divides a figure into two congruent parts that match exactly is a ▢ .

3 A figure that is rotated less than 360° about a point and looks the same as it did before the turn has ▢ .

4 A ▢ can have more than one line of symmetry.

Concepts and Skills

Solve. Which of the dotted lines are lines of symmetry?

5
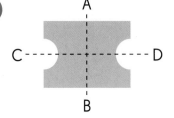

6
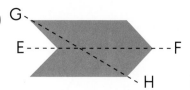

7
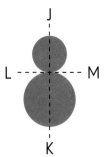

8
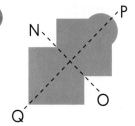

Decide which of these figures have rotational symmetry. Use yes or no.

9

10

Decide which of these figures have rotational symmetry. Use yes or no.

11

12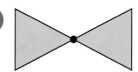

**Each figure shows half of a symmetric shape or pattern.
The dotted line is a line of symmetry of the figure. Copy each figure on
grid paper and complete it. Decide which of these figures
have rotational symmetry. Use ✔ or ✗.**

13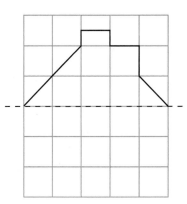

Rotational symmetry:

14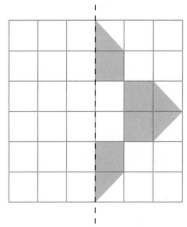

Rotational symmetry:

**Create a symmetric pattern about these lines of symmetry on grid paper.
Use only ▮ and ◣.**

15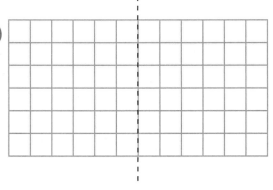

16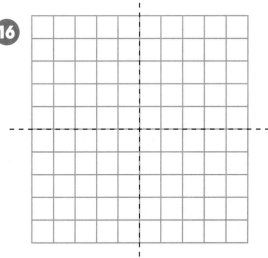

14 Tessellations

The pattern on this shirt is a tessellation.

This is the shape that is repeated to make the tessellation on this tablecloth.

The pattern on the soccer ball is also a tessellation.

This repeated pattern is formed by using two shapes.

The soccer net shows a tessellation. The repeated shape is a hexagon.

Lessons

14.1 Identifying Tessellations

14.2 More Tessellations

BIG IDEA

▶ A tessellation is made when a shape (or shapes) is repeated, covering a plane (or surface) without gaps or overlaps to form patterns.

Recall Prior Knowledge

Drawing shapes on dot paper

Making patterns with shapes

Draw these shapes on dot paper.

1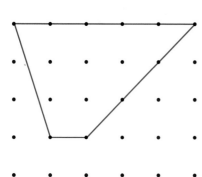

2

Complete each pattern.

3

4

 14.1 Identifying Tessellations

Lesson Objectives

- Recognize and make tessellations.
- Identify the unit shape used in a tessellation.

Vocabulary

tessellation

repeated shape

slide

rotate

flip

Learn Repeat shapes to make patterns.

Look at the picture. It shows part of a floor covered with rectangular tiles.

Look at these shapes.

These shapes can be used to cover a surface with no gaps between them.

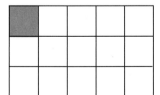 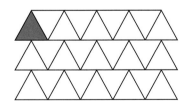 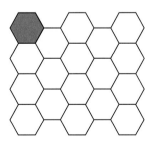

These patterns are called **tessellations**.
A tessellation can be made using a single **repeated shape**.

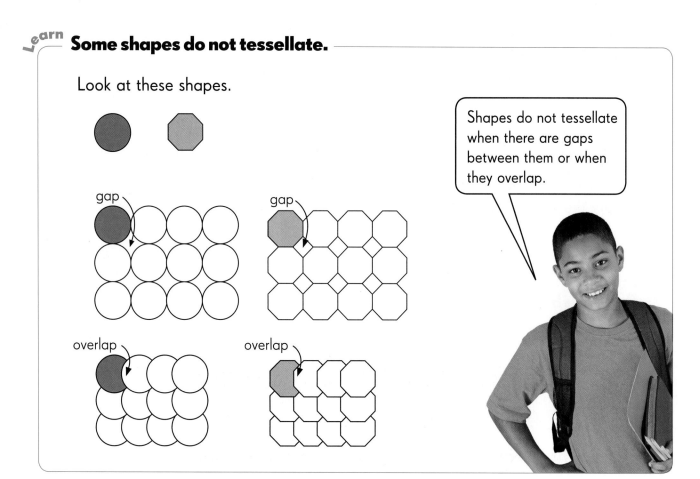

Learn Some shapes do not tessellate.

Look at these shapes.

gap

gap

overlap

overlap

> Shapes do not tessellate when there are gaps between them or when they overlap.

Guided Practice

Copy, identify, and color the repeated shape used in each tessellation.

1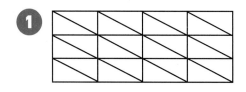

2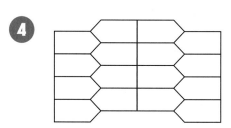

3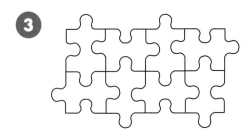

4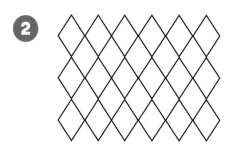

Learn Repeat shapes to form tessellations.

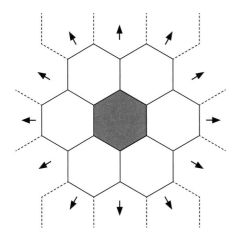

You can form a tessellation by repeating the shape in all directions.

Learn Repeat shapes in different ways to form tessellations.

You can repeat in several ways to form a tessellation.

a You can **slide** the shape.

b You can **rotate** the shape.

Clockwise rotation:

Counter-clockwise rotation:

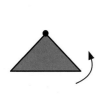   

Continued on next page

c You can **flip** the shape.

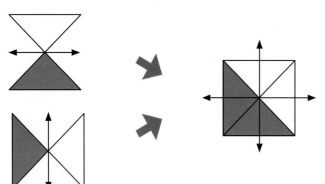

Guided Practice

Identify how each shape was moved. Choose slide, rotate, or flip.

5

6

7

Learn **Repeat shapes in more ways to form tessellations.**

You can flip, then rotate the shape.

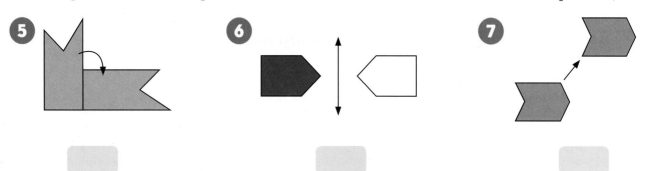

Hands-On Activity

Material:
• dot paper

WORK IN PAIRS

Use ten copies of each shape.

1 Identify the shapes that tessellate.

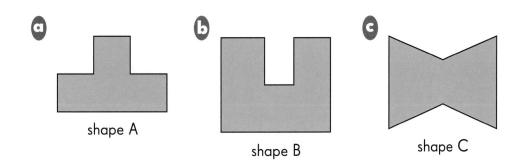

ⓐ

shape A

ⓑ

shape B

ⓒ

shape C

2 Use dot paper to identify the shapes that tessellate.

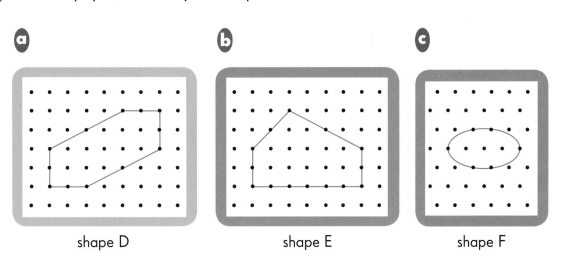

ⓐ

shape D

ⓑ

shape E

ⓒ

shape F

Guided Practice

Copy each shape on dot paper. Make a tessellation with each shape. Use slide, flip, or rotate to explain how you tessellated the shape.

8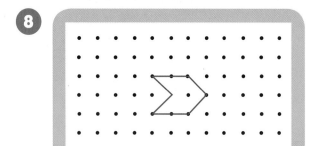

9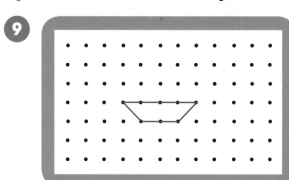

Let's Explore!

Tech Connection

WORK IN PAIRS

STEP 1 Use the computer drawing tool to draw a triangle and make twelve copies of the triangle.

STEP 2 Print and cut out the triangles. Mark the angles as shown. Your triangle can be different from the one shown below.

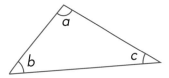

STEP 3 Tessellate the triangles.

Can all triangles tessellate?

Copy, identify, and color the repeated shape used in each tessellation.

 1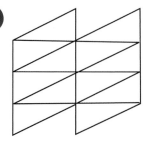

2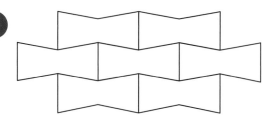

Copy each shape on dot paper. Make a tessellation with each shape.

3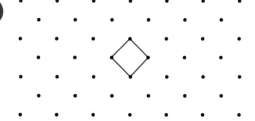

4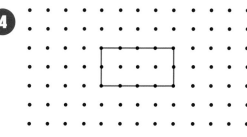

5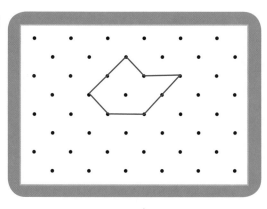

6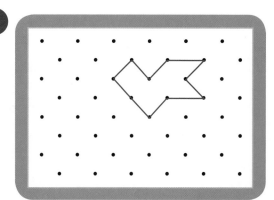

ON YOUR OWN

Go to Workbook B:
Practice 1, pages 133–138

14.2 More Tessellations

Vocabulary
modify

Lesson Objective

- Tessellate shapes in different ways.

ᴸᵉᵃʳⁿ **Tessellate shapes in different ways.**

Here are some ways this shape [ ] tessellates.

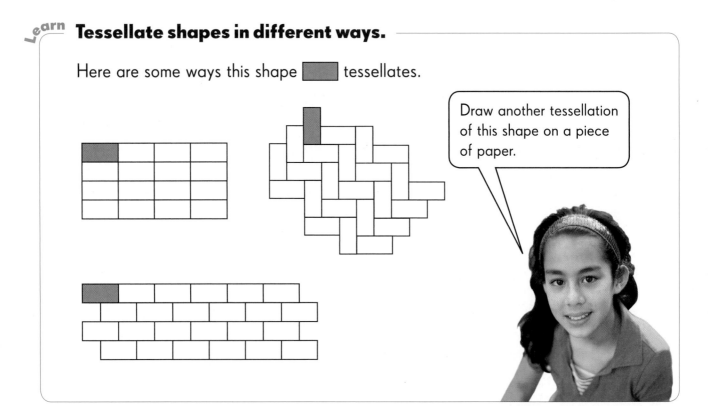

Draw another tessellation of this shape on a piece of paper.

ᴸᵉᵃʳⁿ **Tessellate shapes in more ways to form different tessellations.**

You can rotate, then flip the shape.

You can slide, then rotate the shape.

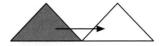 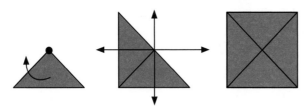 

Guided Practice

Copy the shape on dot paper. Tessellate the shape in another way.

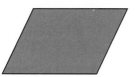

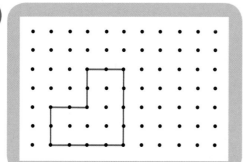

🖐 Hands-On Activity

Materials:
• shape worksheet
• dot paper

1 Use ten copies of each shape.

Tessellate each shape in two different ways.

a

b

2 Copy each shape on dot paper.

Make as many different tessellations as you can for each shape.

a

b

Learn **Modify shapes to make tessellations.**

Cassie designed a pattern for an art competition. She modified a square to create the repeated shape for the tessellation.

Step 1   **Step 2**

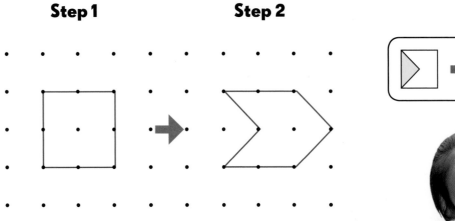

She cut out the shape and made copies of it. She colored half of the shapes blue and the other half of the shapes yellow. Then she repeated the shape to make a tessellation.

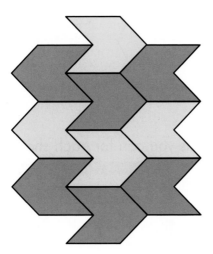

More ways to modify shapes to make tessellations.

Cassie decided to create a second design using a different shape.

Step 1   **Step 2**   **Step 3**

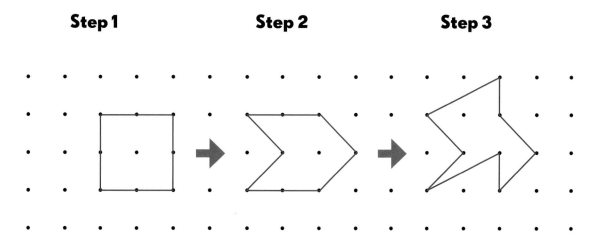

She cut out the shape and made copies of it.
Then she colored the shapes and repeated them
to make another tessellation.

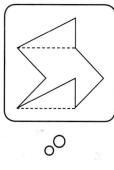

Continued on next page

Ben showed how he designed the repeated shape for his tessellation.

Step 1   **Step 2**   **Step 3**

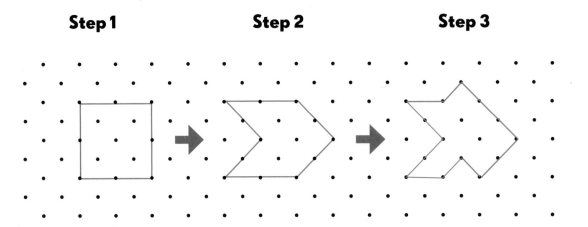

Ben repeated the shape to make his tessellation.

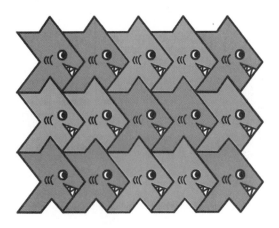

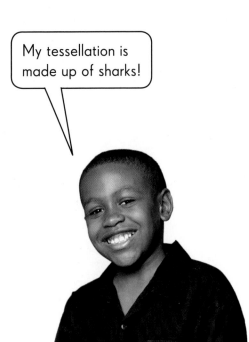

My tessellation is made up of sharks!

Cassie and Ben both designed shapes from a square. The square tessellates, so the new shapes also tessellate.

Hands-On Activity

Material:
• dot paper

Design a shape that tessellates
and make your own tessellation.
Start with a figure that tessellates,
such as one of the shapes below.

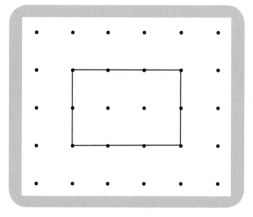

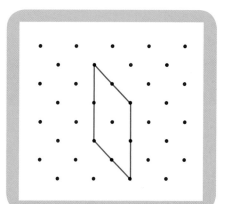

Guided Practice

Modify each shape to make a new shape.
Then make a tessellation for each new shape.

2
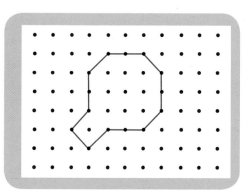

3
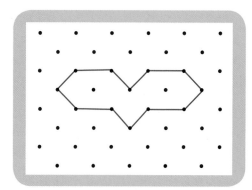

Copy each shape on dot paper.
Tessellate each shape in at least two different ways.

1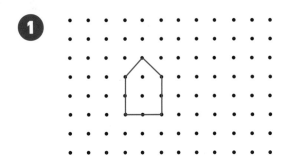

2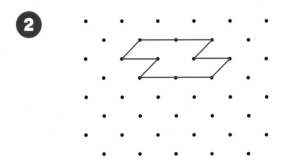

3 Start with any shape that tessellates and design a new shape.

a Use the new shape to make a tessellation.
Compare your tessellation with those of your friends.

b Can you use this shape to make another tessellation?

ON YOUR OWN

Go to Workbook B:
Practice 2, pages 139–142

Describe how the second shape is created from the rectangle.
Does it matter how you modify the shape?
Will all modified shapes still tessellate?
Which modifications allow the shape to continue to tessellate
and which do not?

CRITICAL THINKING SKILLS
Put On Your Thinking Cap!

PROBLEM SOLVING

Tech Connection

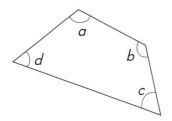

WORK IN PAIRS

STEP 1 Use the computer drawing tool to draw any four-sided figure and make twelve copies of it. Your four-sided figure can be different from the one shown.

STEP 2 Print and cut out the shapes. Then mark the four angles as shown.

STEP 3 Make a tessellation with the shapes.
Does your figure tessellate?
Why or why not? Explain your answer.

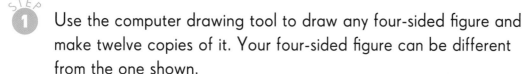

ON YOUR OWN

**Go to Workbook B:
Put on Your Thinking Cap!
pages 143–146**

Chapter Wrap Up

Study Guide

You have learned...

How Tessellations are Formed

A tessellation can be made using a single repeated shape.
This shape covers a surface by extending in all directions with

- no gaps.
- no overlaps.

Identify Shapes to Make Tessellations

Identify the repeated shape in a tessellation.

Recognize shapes that
- tessellate.
- do not tessellate.

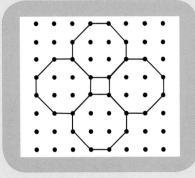

Tessellations can be formed by
- sliding shapes.

- rotating shapes.

- flipping shapes.

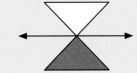

Tessellations

BIG IDEA

▶ A tessellation is made when a shape (or shapes) is repeated, covering a plane (or surface) without gaps or overlaps to form patterns.

Make Tessellations from Given Shapes

Draw tessellations with a given shape on dot paper.

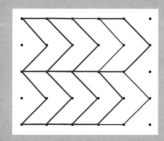

Make different tessellations with a given shape.

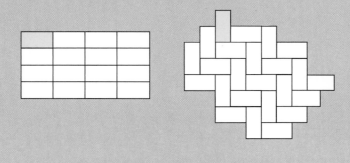

Modify Shapes to Form New Tessellations

Use a shape that can tessellate to design a new shape that can tessellate.

Chapter Review/Test

Vocabulary

Choose the correct word.

| tessellation |
| repeated |
| slide |
| rotate |
| flip |
| modify |

1 When any number of a shape can be fitted together to cover a surface without any gaps or overlaps, a _____ is formed.

2 A tessellation can be made using a single _____ shape.

3 To form a tessellation with a given shape, you can _____ or _____ or _____ it.

4 You can _____ a repeated shape to create a new shape that can tessellate.

Concepts and Skills

Identify the repeated shape used to form this tessellation.

5

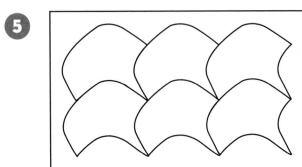

6 **Copy each shape on dot paper. Identify the shapes that do not tessellate.**

a

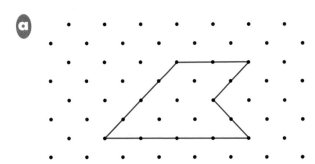

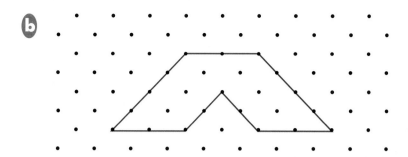

Copy the shape on dot paper to make two different tessellations.

7 Tessellation 1

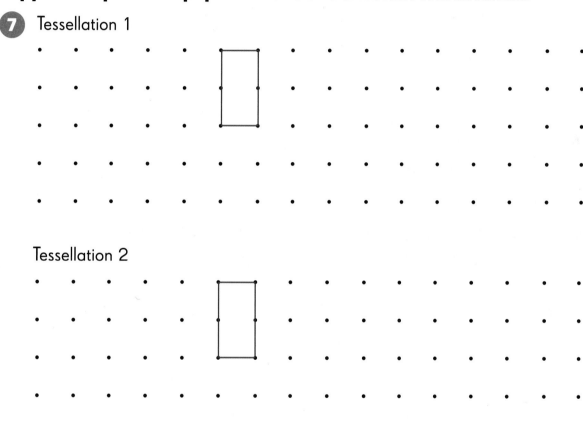

Tessellation 2

Draw the shape on dot paper. Modify the shape to create a new shape. Then tessellate the new shape.

8

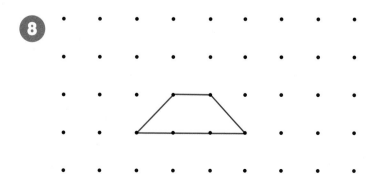

Glossary

- **acute angle**

  An angle with a measure less than 90°.

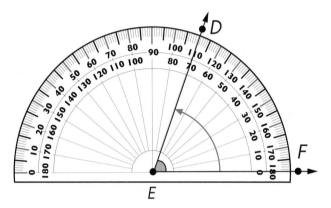

  ∠*DEF* is an acute angle.

- **angle**

  When two rays share the same endpoint, they form an angle.

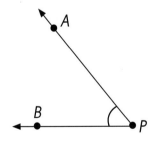

  $\overrightarrow{PA}$ and $\overrightarrow{PB}$ meet to form ∠*APB*.

- **angle measure**

  See *degrees*.

- **area**

  Area is the amount of surface covered by a figure.
  Area can be measured in square units such as
  square centimeter (cm^2), square meter (m^2), square inch ($in.^2$),
  square foot (ft^2), square yard (yd^2), and square mile (mi^2).

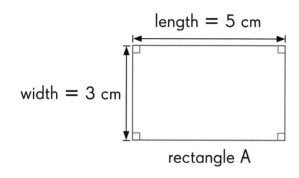

length = 5 cm

width = 3 cm

rectangle A

Area of rectangle = length × width
= 5 × 3
= 15 cm^2
The area of rectangle A is
15 square centimeters.

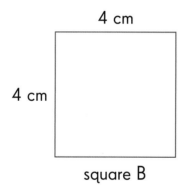

4 cm

4 cm

square B

Area of square = length of side ×
length of side
= 4 × 4
= 16 cm^2
The area of square B is
16 square centimeters.

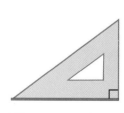

- **base (of a drawing triangle)**

The straightedge is at the base of the drawing triangle.

C

- ## clockwise

  A rotation in the same direction as the hands on a clock.

- ## center of rotation

  See *rotate*.

- ## congruent

  Identical parts of figures are congruent. They have the same shape and size.

  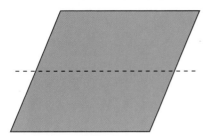

- ## composite figure

  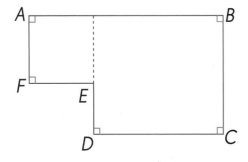

  Figure *ABCDEF* is a composite figure. It can be broken up into a square and a rectangle.

- ## counter-clockwise

  A rotation in the opposite direction as the hands on a clock.

D

- **decimal**

  A decimal is a way to show amounts that are parts of a whole. A decimal is a number with a decimal point to the right of the ones place, and digits to the right of the decimal point.

  1.52 is a decimal.

- **decimal form**

  1 tenth written in decimal form is 0.1.

- **decimal point**

  A dot or symbol separating the ones and tenths places in a decimal.

  0.1

  decimal point

- **degrees (in angles)**

  A unit of angle measure. An angle measure is a fraction of a full turn. The symbol for degrees is °.

  A right angle has a measure of 90 degrees. It can be written as 90°.

- **drawing triangle**

  An instrument used to draw perpendicular and parallel line segments.

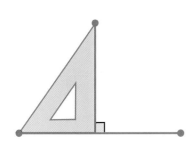
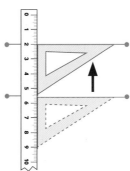

E

- ## endpoint

  The point at the beginning of a ray or at either end of a line segment.

  ray *AB* or $\overrightarrow{AB}$

  line segment *EF* or $\overline{EF}$

- ## equivalent fraction

  Equivalent fractions have the same value.

  $\frac{2}{3}$ and $\frac{10}{15}$ are equivalent fractions.

- ## expanded form

  The expanded form of a number shows the number as the sum of the values of its digits.

  $1.46 = 1 + 0.4 + 0.06$

  $1 + 0.4 + 0.06$ is the expanded form of 1.46.

F

- ## flip

  Turn a shape front to back over a line.

  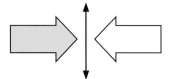

- ## greater than (>)

  Place-value charts can be used to compare decimals.

Ones		Tenths	Hundredths
0		4	
0		3	4

  0.4 is greater than 0.34.

- ## greatest

Ones		Tenths	Hundredths
0		6	2
0		2	3
0		6	0

  The greatest decimal is 0.62.

- ## horizontal lines

  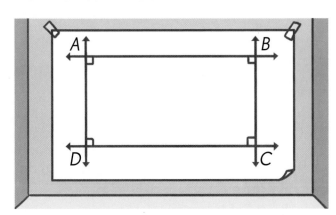

  $\overleftrightarrow{AB}$ and $\overleftrightarrow{DC}$ are horizontal lines.

- **hundredth**

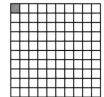

One part out of a hundred is $\frac{1}{100}$ (one hundredth).

- **inner scale (of a protractor)**

The inner set of readings on a protractor used for measuring angles.

Since $\overrightarrow{EF}$ passes through the zero mark of the inner scale, read the measure on the inner scale.

Measure of $\angle DEF = 70°$

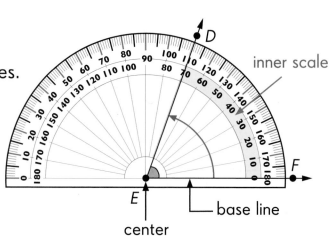

inner scale

base line

center

- **least**

Ones	Tenths	Hundredths
0	6	2
0	2	3
0	6	0

The least decimal is 0.23.

- **length**

The distance along a line segment or figure from one point to another. It is usually the longer side of a rectangle.

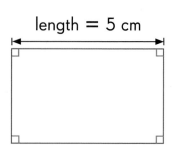

length = 5 cm

- **less than (<)**

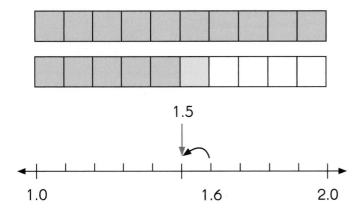

1.5 is 0.1 less than 1.6.

- **line**

  A line is a straight path continuing without end in two opposite directions. Write line *CD* or *DC* as $\overleftrightarrow{CD}$ or $\overleftrightarrow{DC}$.

- **line segment**

  A line segment is part of a line with two endpoints. Write line segment *EF* or *FE* as $\overline{EF}$ or $\overline{FE}$.

- **line of symmetry**

  A line that divides a figure into two congruent parts. The parts match exactly when folded along this line.

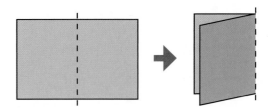

- **line symmetry**

  If a figure can be folded in half so that the halves match exactly, the figure has line symmetry.

M

- **modify (a shape)**

  Create a new shape for a tessellation.

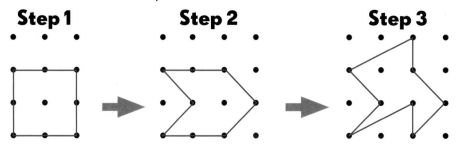

- **more than**

0.7 is 0.1 more than 0.6.

O

- **obtuse angle**

  An angle with a measure greater than 90° but less than 180°.

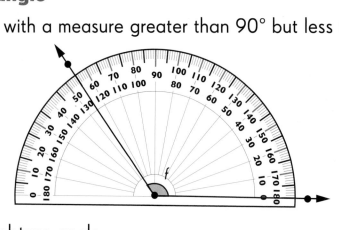

∠f is an obtuse angle.

- **order**

  To order a set of numbers is to arrange them in a sequence following a set of rules.

- **outer scale (of a protractor)**

  The outer set of readings on a protractor used for measuring angles.

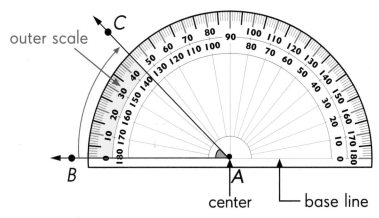

Since $\overrightarrow{AB}$ passes through the zero mark of the outer scale, read the measure on the outer scale.

Measure of $\angle CAB = 45°$

P————————

- **parallel line segments (||)**

  Parallel line segments are always the same distance apart.

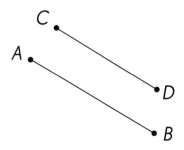

$\overline{AB} \parallel \overline{CD}$

- **perimeter**

  Perimeter is the distance around a figure. Perimeter can be measured in units such as centimeter (cm), meter (m), inch (in.), foot (ft), yard (yd), and mile (mi).

  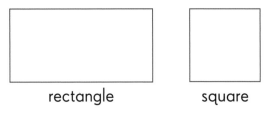

  rectangle   square

  Perimeter of rectangle = length + width + length + width
  Perimeter of square = 4 × length of side

- **perpendicular line segments (⊥)**

  Line segments that meet at right angles.

  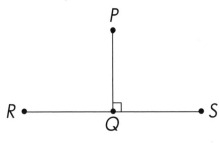

  $\overline{PQ} \perp \overline{RS}$

- **placeholder zero**

  Decimals can have placeholder zeros.
  The digit zero to the right of 9 tenths is a placeholder zero.

  0.9<u>0</u> has the same value as 0.9.

  $$0.9\underline{0} = \frac{90}{100}$$
  $$= \frac{9}{10}$$
  $$= 0.9$$

- **protractor**

   An instrument used to measure and draw angles.

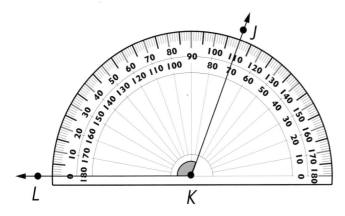

R————————————

- **ray**

   A ray is part of a line that continues without end in one direction.
   It has one endpoint.

   Letters can be used to name a ray. The first letter is always the endpoint.

   A ————————→ B   B ————————→ A
   ray *AB*   ray *BA*

   Ray *AB* can also be written as $\overrightarrow{AB}$, and ray *BA* as $\overrightarrow{BA}$.

- **rectangle**

   A rectangle is a four-sided figure with opposite
   sides parallel, and of equal length.
   It has four right angles.

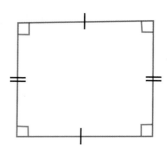

- **repeated shape**

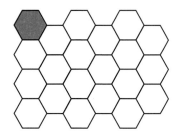

The repeated shape in this tessellation is .

- **right angle**

An angle that measures exactly 90°.

- **rotate**

The change in position that occurs when a shape is turned about a point. This point is called the *center of rotation*.

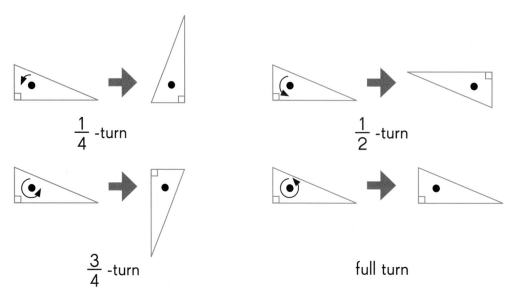

$\frac{1}{4}$ -turn $\qquad\qquad$ $\frac{1}{2}$ -turn

$\frac{3}{4}$ -turn $\qquad\qquad$ full turn

- **rotational symmetry**

A figure has rotational symmetry if it can be rotated less than a full turn (360°) around a center and look the same as it did before the turn.

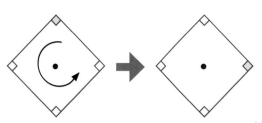

- **round (in decimals)**

To round a decimal is to express it to the nearest whole number, tenth, and so on.

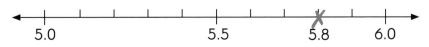

5.8 rounded to the nearest whole number is 6.

- **slide**

Move a figure in any direction to a new position.

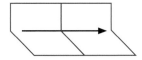

- **square**

A square is a four-sided figure with four right angles and all sides of equal length. It is a special type of rectangle.

See *rectangle*.

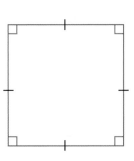

- **square units**

Units such as square centimeter (cm^2), square meter (m^2), square inch ($in.^2$), square foot (ft^2), square yard (yd^2), and square mile (mi^2) are used to measure area.

- **straight angle**

An angle with a measure of 180°.

- **symmetric figure (in line symmetry)**

A figure with two congruent parts that match along the line of symmetry. A figure can have more than one line of symmetry.

T

- ## tenth

One part out of ten is $\frac{1}{10}$ (one tenth).

- ## tessellation

A tessellation can be made using any number of a single repeated shape fitted together to cover a surface without any gap or overlap.

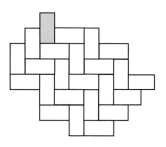

- ## turns (and right angles)

1 right angle

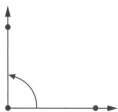

A $\frac{1}{4}$-turn is 90°.

2 right angles

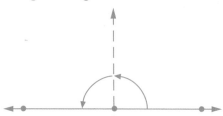

A $\frac{1}{2}$-turn is 180°.

3 right angles

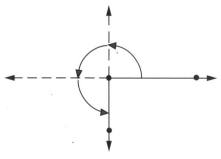

A $\frac{3}{4}$-turn is 270°.

4 right angles

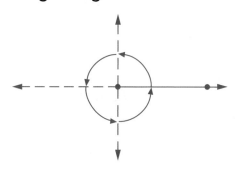

A full turn is 360°.

V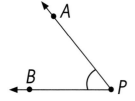

- **vertex**

  The point at which two line segments, or rays meet to form an angle.

  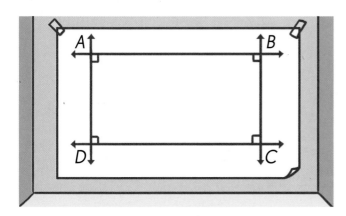

  Point *P* is called the vertex.

- **vertical lines**

  $\overleftrightarrow{AD}$ and $\overleftrightarrow{BC}$ are vertical lines.

W

- **width**

  Usually the shorter side of a rectangle.

  width = 3 cm

  See *length*.

Index

Pages listed in regular type refer to Student Book A.
Pages in blue type refer to Student Book B.
Pages in *black italic* type refer to Workbook (WB) A pages.
Pages in *blue italic* type refer to Workbook (WB) B pages.
Pages in **boldface** type show where a term is introduced.

Pages listed in regular type refer to Student Book A.
Pages in blue type refer to Student Book B.
Pages in *black italic* type refer to Workbook (WB) A pages.
Pages in *blue italic* type refer to Workbook (WB) B pages.
Pages in **boldface** type show where a term is introduced.

Lines
symbol for, 85
horizontal, 119–124; *WB 65–68*
parallel, 106–108, 119–118, 199–120
perpendicular, 106–108, 119–120
of symmetry, 197–202, 208–212, 215–217;
WB 123–124
vertical, 119–124; *WB 65–68*

Line graph, **140**
interpreting, 140–144, 150, 158; *WB 75–77, 79–80,
89–90*
making, 145
reading, 140–144, 150, 158; *WB 75–77, 79–80,
89–90*
using, 140–144, 148–150, 158; *WB 75–77, 79–80,
89–90*

Line plot, **176**, 178–182, 184–186, 207, 214; *WB 104,
106–108, 124–126, 171, 177*

Line of symmetry, **197**–202, 208–212, 215–217;
WB 123–124

Line symmetry, **197**–202, 208–212, 215–217;
WB 123–124

Line segment
parallel and perpendicular, 106, 109–118, 120–124;
WB 61–67
symbol for, 85; *WB 61–67*

Make predictions, 192–195, 197, 201–203, 209–210;
WB 113–114, 129–130, 172, 177

Manipulatives
chip models, 5–7, 9–10, 12, 77–79, 82, 86, 96–99
classroom objects, 9, 17, 170–171, 192–194, 197,
200, 202
connecting cubes, 166, 196
counters, 12
drawing triangle, 112–116, 121, 124; *WB 63–64,
66–67*
fraction circles, 231, 240
geoboards, 133, 135, 156, 168
measuring tape, 39
number cubes, 82, 246
place-value blocks, 71–75, 77

protractor, 88–97, 102, 104; *WB 47–54*
straightedge, 111–118, 121–122, 124, *WB 63–64,
66–67*
ruler, 106
spinners, 194–195, 198–199, 209; *WB 115*

Math Journal, *See* Communication

Mean, **165**, 166–173, 177, 181–183, 185–186,
204–208, 212–213, 215, 218–219; *WB 93–100,
107–112, 119–126, 132–133, 135–136, 171,
176–177*

Measures of central tendency, 204, *See also* Mean, Median,
Mode, and Range

Median, **174**, 175–177, 180, 183–186, 188–191,
206–208, 218; *WB 101–104, 106, 109–112,
122–128, 171–172, 178*

Mid-Year Review, *See* Assessment

Mental math, 70

Mixed numbers,
addition with, 230, 232, 250–251, 254, 259–260;
WB 155
as decimals, 44–45, 47, 52; *WB 6, 17–18*
definition of, 230; *WB 141*
improper fractions and, 237–254; *WB 147–154,
174–175*
modeling, 230–232, 234–236, 243–244, 248,
250–252; *WB 141–145, 169, 174*
on a number line, 233–236, 245–247; *WB 144–146,
150*
subtraction with, 252–254, 260–262, 265; *WB 156*

Mode, 178, 179–180, 183–185, 188–191, 206–208,
213–214, 218; *WB 101–104, 106, 109–112, 122–
124, 127–128, 134, 171–172, 177–178*

Models
abstract, *throughout. See for example*, 45, 78–82, 224,
232, 234–241, 243–244, 248, 250–252; *WB 62,
66, 137, 139*
concrete, 166, 192–193, 224, 227, 230–231, 255;
WB 144
geoboard, 133, 135, 156, 168

Pages listed in regular type refer to Student Book A.
Pages in blue type refer to Student Book B.
Pages in *black italic* type refer to Workbook (WB) A pages.
Pages in *blue italic* type refer to Workbook (WB) B pages.
Pages in **boldface** type show where a term is introduced.

Numbers to 100,000
    comparing, 14–20, 22, 32–43, 62; *WB 7–11, 14,
        35–36*
    expanded form, **11**, 12–13, 24–25; *WB 5, 35*
    ordering, **15**, 18; *WB 7–8, 36*
    patterns, **6**, 8, 16, 19; *WB 2, 9, 10, 11, 32, 36*
    standard form, **6**, 7–9, 24–25; *WB 1, 35*
    word form, **6**, 7–9, 24–25; *WB 1, 35*

Number patterns, 6, 8, 16, 19; *WB 2, 9, 10, 11, 32, 36*
    decimals, 26–30, 34, 52; *WB 10, 12*

Number sense
    common multiples, **58**, 59, 61, 68; *WB 29, 33, 39*
    comparing whole numbers, 14–20, 22, 32–34, 62;
        WB 7–11, 14, 35–36
    front-end estimation, *See* Estimation
    interpreting remainders, 37
    multiplication and division, *See* Multiplication and Division

Number sentences
    addition/subtraction, *See* Addition and Subtraction
    bar models and, *See* Bar models
    multiplication/division, *See* Multiplication and Division
    for real-world problems, *See* Algebraic thinking

Number theory
    factors, *See* Factors
    multiples, *See* Multiples
    prime and composite numbers, 50, 51, 54, 68;
        WB 24–26, 39

Numerator of a fraction, **224**

Obtuse angle, **90**–93, 97, 103–104; *WB 48, 53*

Operations, *See* Addition, Division, Multiplication, and
Subtraction

Opposite sides (of a rectangle), 126, 128, 130–132, 137,
    140–141, 145–146; *WB 73-81*

Ordering
    data, 174–175, 177, 183, 186; *WB 101–102,*
        See also Line plot and Stem-and-leaf plot
    whole numbers, **15**, 18; *WB 7–8, 36*
    decimals, 29–30, 34, 52; *WB 12*

Organizing data
    line plot, *See* Line plot

stem-and-leaf plot, *See* Stem-and-leaf plot
    table, 126–139, 145, 154–157; *WB 67–73, 85–88*
    tally chart, 128–129, 131, 155; *WB 67, 69*

Outcomes
    likelihood of, 192–195, 197, 201–203, 209–210;
        WB 113–114, 129–130, 172, 177
    meaning of, **192**
    probability of, 198–203, 210–211, 213–214, 219;
        WB 115–118, 129–131, 136, 173, 179

Outer scale, 88, 90–93, 102–104; *WB 47*

Outlier, **188**, 208–209; *WB 109, 112, 126, 172, 178*

Parallel lines, 106–108, 119, 122

Parallel line segments, 105, 110, 115–118, 120–124;
    WB 63–64, 65–67

Patterns
    completing, 6, 8, 16, 19; *WB 2, 9, 10, 11, 32, 36*
    creating, 16; *WB 9*
    decimals, 26–30, 34, 52; *WB 10, 12*
    extending, 6, 8, 16, 19; *WB 2, 9, 10, 11, 32, 36*
    numerical, 6, 8, 16, 19; *WB 2, 9, 10, 11, 32, 36*
    symmetric, 208, 210–215, 217; *WB 128–129*
    wallpaper, 148

Perimeter
    of a square, 164–165, 167, 169, 190, 192; *WB 95,*
        99–101, 105
    of a rectangle, 163–167, 169, 190, 192; *WB 95, 99,*
        101–102, 105
    of a composite figure, 170–171, 174, 175, 182–183,
        186–188, 191, 193; *WB 107–109, 115*

Perpendicular lines, 106–108, 119, 122

Perpendicular line segments, 105, 110–114, 120–124; *WB*
    61–62, 65–67

Pictographs, 147–150; *WB 78*

Pages listed in regular type refer to Student Book A.
Pages in blue type refer to Student Book B.
Pages in *black italic* type refer to Workbook (WB) A pages.
Pages in *blue italic* type refer to Workbook (WB) B pages.
Pages in **boldface** type show where a term is introduced.

with mixed numbers, *See* Mixed numbers
models, 227–229, 252–254, 260; *WB 139*
sentence, *throughout. See for example* 33–35, 41, 43,
66–67; *WB 15–17, 139–140*

Symmetry, 194–217; *WB 123–129*

Table **128**
interpreting, 128–139, 151, 155–157; *WB 69, 71–73,*
85–88
organizing data in, 126–132, 145, 154–156;
WB 67–70, 85–86

Tally chart, **128**
using, to make a table, 128–129, 131, 155; *WB 67, 69*

Ten thousand, **5**, 6–26; *WB 2–5, 12–14, 35–36, 40*

Tenth, 1, 4–2, 24–79; *WB 1–4*

Tessellation, 218–239; *WB 133–142*

Three-quarter turns, **89**, 98–102, 104; *WB 55–56*

Turn
quarter, 89, 98–102, 104; *WB 55–56*
half, 98–102, 104; *WB 55–56*
three-quarter, 89, 98–102, 104; *WB 55–56*
full, 87, 98–100, 102, 104; *WB 55–56*

Vertex
of an angle, 85-86, 88-97, 102-104; *WB 45–46, 49,*
51

Vocabulary, 5, 14, 24, 32, 44, 56, 66, 86, 96, 101, 118,
126, 134, 140, 154, 165, 174, 187, 192, 198, 204,
218, 224, 230, 237, 243, 272

Vertical axis, **140**

Vertical lines, 119–124; *WB 65–68*

Whole numbers
place value, 5–26, 32–34; *WB 2–5, 7–14, 35–36, 40*
rounding, *See* Estimation
writing, 6–9, 11–13, 24–25; *WB 1, 5, 35*

Width, 152–155, 157, 161, 163–169, 176, 178–186,
187–188, 190, 192–193, *WB 94–106, 111–116*

Word form, **6**, 7–9, 24–25; *WB 1, 35*

Zero
in the quotient, 103, 107; *WB 55*
in decimals, 4–79; *WB 1–18*
placeholder, 17–18; *WB 8, 10, 12, 15–16*

Photo Credits